PRIVATE EYE ANNUAL 2015

EDITED BY IAN HISLOP

Published in Great Britain by
Private Eye Productions Ltd
6 Carlisle Street, London W1D 3BN
www.private-eye.co.uk

© 2015 Pressdram Ltd
ISBN 978-1-901784-63-3
Designed by Bridget Tisdall
Printed and bound in Italy
by L.E.G.O. S.p.A

2 4 6 8 10 9 7 5 3 1

PRIVATE EYE ANNUAL 2015

EDITED BY IAN HISLOP

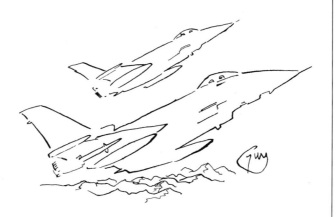

RAF IN MIDDLE EAST MISSION

*"It just seems a long way to come to bomb a load
of blokes from South London"*

THE ENTIRE ELECTION COVERAGE IN FULL

Daily Mail
ED MILIBAND IS WEIRD

DAILY Mirror
DAVID CAMERON IS POSH

THE TIMES
Poll shows Ed Miliband is weird

theguardian
Poll shows David Cameron is posh

The Daily Telegraph
Cressida Bonas thinks Ed Miliband is weird

The INDEPENDENT
Cameron is weird and Ed Miliband is posh

DAILY EXPRESS
NIGEL FARAGE IS NOT WEIRD OR POSH

FINANCIAL TIMES
Markets plunge as Weird/Posh index rises

HOW SCOTLAND WILL LOOK AFTER INDEPENDENCE

'YES' CAMPAIGN

'NO' CAMPAIGN

Scottish Independence
The Big Questions

As the biggest constitutional change in British history looms, the Eye's panel of Scottish experts (Phil McSpace, Sally Jockstrap, Glen Slagg and Peter McHackie) take on the really vital issues for our non-Scottish readers living in the former United Kingdom of Great Britain (FUKOFGB).

Can we now boo Andy Murray?	Yes
Can we boo Andy Murray's mother on Strictly?	Yes
Will Andrew Neill be extradited?	Yes
Can we all just ignore the Edinburgh Fringe?	Yes
Will we have to bail out RBS?	Yes
Can we skip the shipping forecast?	Yes
Will people do charity walks from Land's End to Carlisle?	Yes
Will they build a wall on Hadrian's Wall?	No
Will we have to listen to Alex Salmond ever again?	No
Will the British Bake-Off still include Highland shortbread?	No
Will the Queen have to get a passport to go to Balmoral?	Yes
Will Dr Who need a passport to film in Wales, or will he just go back in time to before independence?	No
Can we just call the Scottish play 'Macbeth' now, luvs?	No
How do you know all this, are you just making it up?	Yes
Is that enough big questions?	Yes, Ed

"The rest is history..."

Exclusive to All Papers
An Apology

IN RECENT months and years, we may have given the mistaken impression that Gordon Brown was an embarrassment, a vainglorious malcontent whose light-touch regulation as Chancellor led directly to the 2007/2008 crash and the deepest recession this country has ever known, a moody, irritable, paranoid man, prone to explosive temper tantrums and whose time as Prime Minister was a disaster.

We now realise, in the light of Gordon Brown being brought in to save the "Better Together" campaign, that nothing could be further from the truth and that Gordon Brown is a colossus of modern politics, bestriding all stripes and parties, loved and respected on all sides of the political divide as a man who doesn't abide fools gladly.

We apologise for any confusion caused and any further confusion when Scotland votes for independence and we again lambast him as an utter disaster.

What you will see on SBS Fox movie channel (formerly BBC Scotland)

Flash Gordon "Gordon's Alive!" Yes, he is and Mr Brown has only 24 hours to save the Unioniverse. Can the ageing Caledonian superhero defeat the Evil Empire, led by Alan CumMing the Merciless, who is clearly on another planet? Soundtrack by Disgruntled Queen.

Highlander There can be only one winner. The film starts in the present and, after independence, ends up in medieval Scotland. Alex Salmond hopes to live forever, by cutting off the head of Britain. Gory and unpleasant, as is the film.

Trainspotting Nightmarish vision of independent Scotland, where there are no trains left to spot and the only traffic is in drugs. Join Fat Boy and his friends as they get high on their own rhetoric and dive down the toilet, taking Scotland with them.

Dr No From his lair on an island in the Caribbean, Sean Connery takes on the evil Dr No, who is set on ruining the world by denying Scotland independence. Don't miss the great scene where Sean tells Miss Moneypenny that from now on she's Miss Moneyeuro.

Salmond Fishing Up the Digger's Arse Alex Salmond attempts the impossible, by fishing for Rupert Murdoch's support. Amusing cameo from a female Sturgeon, flapping around our hero (Mr Murdoch).

A SHORT HISTORY OF THE MOST SUCCESSFUL UNION THE WORLD HAS EVER SEEN

– by Ben MullofKintyre

"So I turned round to him and said..."

How Scotland and England got together

IN THE early 18th century, Scotland was a poor and deprived country which had invested all its remaining money in a huge and bold gamble. It was called the "Darien Scheme" and was going to create huge wealth, which would keep the Scottish people rich and happy for ever.

But, alas, the great gamble didn't work out as they'd planned. Scotland went bankrupt, and was only saved from starvation and disaster when the English came to the rescue and agreed to take on all their debts as part of the two countries uniting as one.

How It All Went Swimmingly

For the next 300 years the English and the Scots worked together to create the world's greatest empire, much of it run by Scotsmen. Together they created the industrial revolution, creating world-beating industries, such as shipbuilding, many of them run by Scotsmen. Together they created the most effective parliamentary government ever known, very often run by Scotsmen.

There is, alas, no space here to mention all the other stupendous joint achievements of these two peoples, in such fields as science, medicine, philosophy, the arts, the law, broadcasting and much else besides.

How It All Went Wrong

In the closing decades of the 20th Century, Scotland sank into a sad state of decline. Its once great industries, such as shipbuilding, disappeared. Its people became increasingly poor and deprived. So they began to dream of taking another huge and bold gamble.

If only they could separate once again from the English, then the Scottish people could be rich and happy for ever.

How It All Ended

In the early 21st Century, the Scots finally screwed up their courage to risk all, by betting everything they had on the so-called "Salmond Scheme".

Inevitably, the great gamble ended in disaster. The newly independent Scotland quickly went bankrupt, wholly unable to pay its mountain of debts.

Before long, a delegation of Scots came to London to ask the English to bail them out. They also wondered, as part of the deal, if they might be interested in forming a political union between their two countries, which might possibly last for at least 300 years.

TIME FOR SALMOND

It's 13.14

WHY IS THE 'NO' CAMPAIGN SO NEGATIVE?

It is trying to convince people to vote No.
Er...
That's it.

The Adventures of Mr Milibean

Fountain & Jamieson

SALTIRED NUTS AHOY! MILIBEAN'S NORTH OF THE BORDER!

SCOTLAND IS TOO SMALL AND INSIGNIFICANT TO EXIST ON ITS OWN!

TO GET WHAT IT WANTS, IT HAS TO HAVE THE CONTINUING SUPPORT OF A MUCH LARGER NEIGHBOUR!

TAKE IT FROM ONE WHO KNOWS..!

HENRY DAVIES

7

Let's Parlez Franglais!
au Summit de NATO
avec Président Hollande

Les most important personnes du monde – et David Cameron

M. Obama *(pour c'est lui)*: Okey dokey, mes amis. Nous êtes finalement en agreement…que Cardiff est un vrai dump.

Tout le monde *(sauf Frau Merkel, qui ne comprend pas le joke)*: Ha ha ha ha.

M. Obama: Mais sérieusement, nous agreeons on que faire about l'Organisation de terreur qui s'appelle "ISIL".

M. Cameron: Non, non, non. C'est ISIS, come le jolly old rivière dans Oxford.

Frau Merkel: Nein, nein. L'organisation s'appelle IS!

M. Hollande: Ooh la la! Nous n'avons pas un agreement après all. What were nous thinking?!

M. Obama *(holding up le livre par Madame Rottweiler)*: Well, Monsieur Hollande! Nous tous know what vous are thinking about toujours le temps. Et ce n'est pas le situation dans le Middle East.

M. Cameron: C'est quelque chose far hotter!

Tout le monde *(sauf Frau Merkel)*: Ha ha ha ha.

M. Hollande: Sacré bleu! C'est un très sérieux matter, et pas quelque chose pour sniggering about. Nous avons need to venir à un agreement.

M. Obama: Okay. Nous tous agree que votre leg-over antics sont vraimant amusants. Et nous ne pouvons pas wait for le sequel.

M. Cameron: Qui va jouer you dans le film? Danny De Vito?

Tout le monde *(sauf Frau Merkel)*: Ha ha ha ha.

M. Obama: Anyway, qui va payer pour notre next petite guerre dans le Middle East? Nous n'avons pas any money.

M. Hollande et M. Cameron: Nous n'avons un bean either.

Frau Merkel *(seulement)*: Ha ha ha ha.

M. Obama: Bon, if nous sommes finis, je vais to Stonehenge pour mon Bucket List. Au revoir.

EXCLUSIVE TO ALL PAPERS

Reeva Steenkamp found guilty of going to toilet

by Our Murder Staff
Gill Tee

IN A dramatic end to the Oscar Pistorius murder trial, a South African judge has found his dead girlfriend Reeva Steenkamp guilty of going to the toilet in the middle of the night.

"Having listened to all the evidence and heard how Oscar Pistorius shot Reeva dead, I definitely find the young woman guilty of going to the toilet without all due care and attention," said Judge Masipa.

"How could she have been so reckless as not to have shaken Oscar awake before going to the loo, knowing he would of course assume the noise of her in the toilet was a heavily armed gang of black youths invading the house?

"It is far too much to have expected a famous person like Oscar to have called out, 'Is that you, Reeva?', or for him to have felt the pillow next to him to see if she was there, before he fired four bullets in self-defence, not meaning to kill anyone through that toilet door."

POLICE LOG

Neasden Central Police Station

Monday

0500 hrs Inspector Dawn Raid briefs Armed Response Unit and Anti-Terrorism Squad on forthcoming swoop on home of terror suspect operating under name of H. Mantel, living at 1540 Cromwell Avenue. All officers were supplied with tasers, bullet-proof jackets and copies of a book of "short stories", one of which is clearly a detailed blueprint for the assassination of the Prime Minister of Britain, a Mrs M. Thatcher.

0537 hrs Officers surround the suspect's home and effect entry by removing door with explosives. Inside, a middle-aged woman, admitting to name "Mantel" and claiming to be a professional "writer", refuses to admit offences under Incitement to Hatred Act 2006, despite clear evidence to the contrary. After some discussion, Inspector Dawn Raid states "This is not a f***ing book programme, darling," and tasers the suspect with 50,000 volts.

0614 hrs Before completing the arrest procedures, officers are unfortunately called away to attend an emergency incident in the Marie Stopes delivery unit at Queen Mary Seacole Hospital in Lidl Grove. A 20-man Swat team is required to assist council social workers in removing a newborn baby from a suspected unsuitable teenage mother.

0702 hrs When mother proves uncooperative at removal of baby, it is necessary to **(the rest of this log entry has been redacted on the orders of a High Court Judge whom we cannot name for legal reasons)**

0752 hrs Station answerphone cleared of 223 messages from members of public requesting assistance for alleged offences, including rape, burglary, GBH, murder and plot to blow up the Houses of Parliament. Due to lack of resource, it was not possible to respond to these non-urgent requests.

BRITAIN RESPONDS TO GREATEST SECURITY THREAT EVER

by Our Military Staff **General Lack-of-Enthusiasm**

AS the nation faced the gravest external peril of its entire history, the Prime Minister responded forcefully with an immediate declaration of war on the Islamic State.

"Make no mistake," said David Cameron, "We are rising to this unprecedented challenge to our very existence and we are sending six aircraft to Iraq, some of which work, to seek out the jihadis, return to base and then take off again to seek them out again and hopefully bomb them at some point."

"Even the thought of this extraordinary commitment of devastating UK firepower will stop the 30,000 extremist fighters in their tracks – unless the tracks lead into Syria, in which case we will obviously leave them alone."

When asked whether there would be any missile attacks he replied, "You'll have to ask the leaders of the Caliphate, but let's hope they can't read the instruction manuals we left which are all in English."

2014 TURNER PRIZE GOES TO OUTSIDER

by Our Arts Correspondent
PERRYGRAYSON WORSTHORNE

The art world was in raptures last night when the Turner Prize judges unanimously chose the Middle Eastern terrorist co-operative ISIS as this year's winner.

The ISIS entry, entitled *Death To The Infidel*, comprised a series of installation videos showing people having their heads cut off.

The judges declared, "The world has never before seen an artwork so imaginatively conceived and so skilfully executed.

"This video sequence has a raw power and a 'cutting edge' energy that represents the very best of everything the Turner Prize was set up to promote – ie, it is shocking, disturbing, outrageous, sick, and not art at all."

Farage defends Murdoch meeting

by Our Political Correspondent
Pat Ronage

Nigel Farage has insisted there was nothing untoward about his private meeting with Rupert Murdoch, saying he used it to explain to Mr Murdoch that he wasn't like other politicians.

"Whereas other politicians are falling all over themselves to meet with Rupert Murdoch, I made it clear to Rupert Murdoch in our meeting that I would be doing nothing of the sort," said the UKIP leader.

"I told Rupert Murdoch I was in no hurry to meet him, as I'm not like other politicians, and would he please pour me a very large glass of Scotch and tell me what to do?"

Rupert Murdoch later tweeted that he was impressed by Nigel Farage, saying how unlike all the other politicians on his payroll Farage was.

MURDOCH: 'PAGE 3 GIRLS MIGHT BE CLOTHED IN FUTURE'

News Corp loves a cover-up

9

PRESIDENT ASSAD OF SYRIA AN APOLOGY

FROM PRESIDENT OBAMA

IN COMMON with all other world leaders, I may in recent years have given the impression that I felt that President Assad of Syria was in some way not wholly suitable to be a leader of his country. On a number of occasions I may, for instance, have described him as "the most evil man in history", "worse than Hitler", and a "genocidal psychopath who has become a serious threat to world peace".

Such diplomatic cut-and-thrust may have reinforced the view that the US government would have been happy to see President Assad removed from office.

In the light of the rise of the Islamic State, I now realise that there was not a shred of truth to support the above, and that, on the contrary, President Assad is the last bulwark of our civilisation against Islamo-fascist terrorism and the only responsible and trustworthy leader left in the Middle East to help in defending us all against the most evil men in history, who are genocidal psychopaths worse than Hitler, and who have become a serious threat to world peace.

On a personal note, I would like to apologise to my old friend Bashar, who really is one of the good guys, and I'm sure we can work together in the cause of creating a better world.

ON OTHER PAGES:
● Apology to President Rouhani of Iraq 3 ● Apology to Saudis for fact that they now have to use their own weapons to fight a war instead of merely using them as a way to funnel backhanders to themselves, as per usual 94

MILIBAND'S HISTORIC '10-YEAR PLEDGE' TO THE NATION

by Our Political Staff
Quentin Lettshaveanotherlaughatedmiliband

IN HIS keynote speech to the Labour Conference, Mr Ed Miliband astonished delegates by forgetting to say what his spin doctors had been telling everyone for days he was going to say.

The passage Mr Miliband forgot to remember had been billed as the centrepiece of his speech.

His plan had been to make a "covenant with the voters", based on three "solemn and binding pledges".

Those pledges in full

1. Over the next 10 years, I promise that I will do everything I can to look vaguely like a human being.

2. Over the next 10 years, I solemnly swear that I will do everything I can to avoid looking like a complete loser who can't even remember his speech.

3. Over the next 10 years, I resolutely pledge that I will work ceaselessly and round-the-clock to conceal the fact that I have forgotten everything I was going to say about everything that's important.

Ukip Survives Biggest Crisis Yet

by Our News Staff **Charlotte Green**

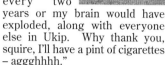

THE United Kingdom Independence Party nearly went into meltdown over the weekend, as millions of supporters attempted to accommodate two conflicting thoughts in their heads at the same time.

"I nearly cracked up," said one Ukip stalwart. "There I was watching the television, when it hit me. I love golf, but I hate Europe. How could I support a European Ryder Cup team playing the greatest game ever invented?"

Wearing a pair of mustard and plum checked trousers, he explained, "At one point I almost cheered on a Spaniard. The whole thing was a nightmare."

He concluded, from the nineteenth hole, "Thank God it only happens once every two years or my brain would have exploded, along with everyone else in Ukip. Why thank you, squire, I'll have a pint of cigarettes – aggghhhh."

But Ukip members were reassured by Paddy Power's Nigel Farage, "So long as the money's right, it's fine to abandon all your principles and support Europe."

Pistorius races into the record books

By our TV Crime staff **A.A. Gillty**

WORLD famous accidental murderer, Oscar Pistorius looks set to enter the history books by setting a new record for the quickest time ever served for careless slaughter.

Said one witness, "It was incredible, when the gun went off you thought the time he was going to do was at least ten years, then it went down to five, but now it looks like he'll have finished in ten months."

When asked if Pistorius would be providing a urine sample, one official said, "To be honest, it might be best if Oscar didn't go anywhere near a toilet."

The Adventures of Mr Milibean

Fountain & Jamieson

DIARY

PIERS MORGAN

MONDAY: Sometimes you just know when you've said something absolutely hilarious.

It happened to me at a star-studded charity event in Leicester tonight. The A-list celebrities were out in full. Bruno Tonioli from Strictly. My old sparring-partner Lord Alan Sugar. Top sports commentator John McCririck. The curvaceous Abi Titmuss. All-round family entertainer Michael Barrymore. The lot.

For some reason – and it can't only have been my ravishing good looks! – all eyes were glued to yours truly.

I was holding court at the top of the table – yes, I've always known my rightful place in this world!

The assembled company were all looking suitably goggle-eyed at my no-punches-pulled tales from The Big Apple, as Hollywood has long been known by insiders.

Bruno Tonioli gasped in delight.

"There's no one quite like you, Piers!" he declared. "You must be one of the funniest men alive!!"

"Less of the 'one of', Bruno!" I quipped back, quick as a flash. At that riposte, the poor guy turned a dark shade of puce.

Memo to Tonioli: if you want to trade witticisms, mate, make sure it's not with the Oscar Wilde *de nos jours*.

And by that I don't mean I prefer blokes to birds of the unfeathered variety – as my gorgeous negligee-wearing wife will testify the next time I execute my marital duties on or about her person!

TUESDAY: To London's exclusive Ivy restaurant, which has re-opened after a massive refurb, paid for by my plentiful ordering of deliciously expensive Bordeaux-style claret wines over the years!

In the corner of the room, I spied Hollywood legend and all-round good bloke George Clooney.

"Glad to see you're able to afford The Ivy, George!" I texted him, cheekily, "Or will you be making your lovely lady wife stick to the Set Menu? Only kidding mate!!!"

I should have remembered that, as cool guys go, George is just about the coolest of them all.

You see, he didn't even look up. In fact, he didn't even pick up his phone.

Instead, he just kept on talking to his charming wife, Amal. And who can blame him? She really is the proverbial 100 percent stunner – and with brains to match.

Later, when I got back to our sumptuous home, I told my own ravishing wife about my oh-so-cheeky text to George Clooney.

"But you don't know him and you haven't got his number!" came her miserable attempt at a put-down.

"Maybe not" I came back, quick as a flash, "But don't tell that to George!"

WEDNESDAY: Tried to get into the swanky exclusive Chiltern Firehouse today, but was told in no uncertain terms that they were "regrettably full up".

Yet another penalty for campaigning so vociferously against USA's crazy gun laws.

Well, I think I can handle it.

Hundreds of thousands of men, women and children have perished as a result of America's refusal to institute gun control.

Personally, I think these innocent lives are more important than the opportunity to dip into the A La Carte menu at an over-rated and over-priced restaurant in an unfashionable corner of London.

I for one am prepared to stand up and be counted, even if that means having the door slammed in my face by the fanatical pro-gun lobby at The Chiltern Firehouse.

Wasn't it James Burke who once said, "The only thing necessary for the triumph of evil is that good men should do nothing"?

THURSDAY: The call came a few weeks ago. Would I stand in for the legendary Nick Owen on BBC1's hugely prestigious Midlands Today?

Respect to BBC Midlands for not caving in to the National Rifle Association. To honour their courage, I accepted the challenge.

Needless to say, the twittersphere literally exploded with excitement. "Piers Morgan on Midlands Today tonight," enthused Jean Young from Derby.

It was a tough gig, but I nailed it. Interviewing 60s pop legend Clodagh Rodgers via exclusive telecommunications application Skype, I was reminded of the time I locked swords with Madonna on my own coast-to-coast CNN show.

"You're a twat!" said the haggard old has-been after I'd mentioned people were saying she was past her best.

"Well, if I'm a twat, what does that make you, Madonna – possibly an even bigger twat!!!" I shot back, a few seconds after she'd left the building.

Needless to say, the other guests laughed fit to bust, or would have done if I could have been bothered to say it out loud.

FRIDAY: The doorbell rings. Guess what? It's my old mates, the Boys in Blue!

"I knew you were coming – I heard it on your phones!" I quip. It's all they can do to stifle their giggles!

Thankfully, I look great in the top-rated handcuffs as I'm led into my own exclusive A-list luxury apartment at the back of their van.

Close friends are already queuing up around the block to witness my debut in the stand in London's prestigious Old Bailey. And mates like Gordon Brown, Simon Cowell, Kevin Pietersen and Amanda Holden are lining up to testify on my behalf – or would be if they could only get back to me!!

Cheers!

As told to
CRAIG BROWN

Fallen angels

"If you want MY opinion, talk of privatisation in the NHS is exaggerated... that'll be £15..."

"The GOOD news is that the number of patients complaining about their care has gone down... the BAD news is that it's because they are all dead!"

"'Whistleblower' isn't a term we're comfortable with... we prefer 'unemployed'"

"The business consultant has ordered a 20% cut in compassion to save money, so I'm afraid you'll have to talk to yourself from now on!"

"Just how much are they paying those agency staff?"

"The new guidelines are for a varied diet, so do you want the pink, slimy stuff or the grey, burnt stuff?"

DUMB BRITAIN

Real contestants, real quiz shows, real answers, real dumb!

The Chase, ITV

Bradley Walsh: On what day of the week did Robinson Crusoe find his companion?
Contestant: Tuesday.

Walsh: The Nun's Priest's Tale is a story by which 14th-century English author?
Contestant: JK Rowling.

Walsh: The title of which Shakespeare play means "everything turns out OK"?
Rugby star: *Macbeth*.

Walsh: What fish are traditionally given as prizes at fairgrounds?
Contestant: Herring.

Walsh: What are people from Jordan called?
Contestant: Saudi Arabian.

Walsh: China have two special administrative regions, Hong Kong and where?
Contestant: Japan.

Walsh: New Zealand was mapped out in the 1770s by which English explorer?
Contestant: Robinson Crusoe.

Walsh: West Indian bowler Michael Holding comes from which country?
Contestant: West India.

Walsh: Which queen of the Iceni led a revolt against the Romans?
Contestant: Elizabeth I.

Walsh: Which queen was the first reigning monarch to send a transatlantic telegram?
Contestant: Elizabeth I.

Walsh: How many wheels did a penny farthing have?
Contestant: Twelve.

Walsh: "Grazie per la musica" is Italian for the title of which Abba song?
Contestant: *Waterloo*.

Walsh: Xenon and what other element contain the letter X in their name?
Contestant: Xylophone.

Walsh: Which of these pairs is named after a French theologian and an English philosopher? Is it (a) Calvin and Hobbes, (b) Wallace and Gromit, or (c) Dastardly and Muttley?
Contestant: Dastardly and Muttley.

Walsh: The Connemara pony is named after an area in which country?
Contestant: India.

Walsh: Which country do Muslims go to on a pilgrimage?
Contestant: Ramadan.

Walsh: Which London mayor supposedly became rich due to his cat's ratting abilities?
Contestant: Boris Johnson.

In It to Win It, BBC1

Dale Winton: Penzance is a town in which English county?
Contestant: I know it's up north somewhere. I'll go for Scotland.

Winton: In Italy what is a trattoria? Is it a policeman, a restaurant or a taxi?
Contestant: It's not a restaurant. It's either a policeman or a taxi. I'll go taxi.

Pointless, BBC1

Alexander Armstrong: The category is famous Williams.
Contestant: I'll take "The Playwright Who Wrote Hamlet". I'm going to say… William Tell.

Armstrong: Name a city beginning with D that stands on the River Liffey.
Contestant: Dunkirk.

Armstrong: We want the names of these historical figures who were all assassinated.
Contestant 1: I'll take "French revolutionary stabbed to death in the bath". Joan of Arc.
Contestant 2: I'm going to have to go with "Assassinated by Lee Harvey Oswald in Dallas". It's JR.

Eggheads, BBC2

Jeremy Vine: In which city is the Ulster museum based?
Contestant: It sounds European. I'm going to go with Brussels.

Two Tribes, BBC2

Richard Osman: Who wrote The Ballad of Reading Gaol after his incarceration there?
Contestant: Gary Glitter.

Osman: Which historic battle in June 1815 marked the end of the Napoleonic wars?
Contestant: The battle of Hastings.

Osman: In the UK, which saint's day is traditionally celebrated on February 14th?
First contestant: St George.
Second contestant: St Alban.

Osman: Since 1997, Whitstable in Kent has been granted protected status under EU legislation for which type of shellfish that is harvested there?
Contestant: Grouse.

Osman: Which exhibition centre in west Kensington shares its name with an ancient site in Greece?
First contestant: Alexandra Palace.
Second contestant: The Royal Albert Hall.

Osman: Which fruit is used to make banoffee pie?
Contestant: Apples.

Tipping Point, ITV

Ben Shephard: Of the seven ancient wonders of the world, what is the only one that is still standing?
Contestant: Is it Mount Everest?

Shephard: What is the capital of the republic of Ecuador?
Contestant: Well, Ecuador's in Spain, so I'll say Barcelona.

Shephard: On what date is Christmas Day traditionally celebrated on each year?
Contestant: Wednesday.

Shephard: Which word links a popular biscuit and a European royal house?
Contestant: My first thought was custard or bourbon, but I'm going to say McVitie's.

Shephard: The name of which Conservative politician is often abbreviated to "IDS"?
Contestant: Margaret Thatcher.

Shephard: In the famous equation $E=mc^2$, what does the "E" stand for?
Contestant: Einstein.

The Link, BBC1

Mark Williams: Which Central American country shares its name with a type of hat?
Contestant: Stetson.

Williams: Bolivia is named in honour of which Simon?
Contestant: Cowell.

Williams: Who is the Italian composer of the operas La Traviata and Aïda?
Contestant: Marconi.

Williams: I attended Downing College, Cambridge, to study law. I was one of the performers on *The Frost Report*. I have played the character Q in a James Bond film. Who am I?
Contestants *(after some discussion):* Arthur Scargill.

Perfection, BBC1

Nick Knowles: True or false, the Sea of Galilee is in Saudi Arabia?
Contestant: I always thought the Sea of Galilee was on the Moon, so I'll say false.

Knowles: Gussie Fink-Nottle was an 18th-century prime minister. True or false?
Contestant: True.

Knowles: The German parliament is known as "The Dummkopf". True or false?
Contestants: We'd like to change Bev's answer from "False" to "True" please.

Fifteen to One, C4

Sandi Toksvig: Born in 1769, what was the name of the first Duke of Wellington?
Contestant: Napoleon Bonaparte.

Toksvig: In which river did John the Baptist baptise Jesus?
Contestant: The Amazon.

Sandi Toksvig: Which British monarch began the tradition of sending telegrams to people celebrating their 100th birthday?
Contestant: Edward III.

Mastermind, BBC1

John Humphrys: According to Thomas Carlyle, Napoleon put down a royalist uprising in Paris, in October 1795, with "a whiff of…" what?
Contestant: Cheese.

Celebrity Mastermind, BBC1

Humphrys: What term for a piece of information that is deliberately misleading comes from a highly smoked fish that was used in the training of hunting dogs, to throw them off the scent?
Georgia Henshaw: Kipper.

Heart Radio, Yorkshire

DJ Dixie: It's like a bigger, fiercer bee,
Caller: Er... spider?
DJ Dixie: No, it still flies and it's yellow and black.
Caller: Oh, er, er... swan?

DUMB FRANCE

Le Maillon Faible, TF1

Host: What is the first name of Cameron, the youngest British PM this century?
Contestant: Cameron Diaz.

SCOTS VOTE NO TO INDEPENDENCE

"The Scottish vote is a total defeat for narrow nationalism..."

"...that's why we need Home Rule for England"

WEDDING OF THE CENTURY

*How the world's most famous couple are descended from British **and** Arab royalty...*

Eye Genealogy Special

King George III	Aladdin
King George the Looney	Amali Baba
King George the Clooney	Amal Anyentob
George the Galloway	Amal Anrubbisher
Gorgeous George Osborne	Muddin Youreye
Prince George the Baby	Amal Nitrate
Wayne Clooney	**Amol Rajan**

Film highlights

Ocean's 94

George Clooney assembles a crack team of A-list Hollywood actors including Brad Pitt, Matt Damon, Bill Murray and Julia Roberts in Venice. As Clooney vows to get himself a good lawyer (Amal Alamuddin) the team use the cover of a glitzy showbiz wedding to pull off an audacious raid to capture the front pages of every newspaper around the world.

"That's quite a feather in your cap"

CLOONEY MARRIES SERIOUS INTERNATIONAL LAWYER

Go on, darling, show us your briefs!

"It's great to be here. I've been living with my parents ever since uni"

EBOLA – A NATION REACTS

The Daily Telegraph
Free Market Will Eventually Defeat Ebola, claims new study

Daily Mail
BBC RESPONSIBLE FOR EBOLA OUTBREAK AND FALLING HOUSE PRICES

THE TIMES
Enough indecision – it is surely time to bomb Ebola before it's too late

London Evening Standard
Top Celebrities With Better Class Of Ebola Than You Photographed At Exclusive West End Nightspot

BuzzFeed
What Strain Of Ebola Have You Got? Take Our Fun Quiz While You Can!

theguardian
Ebola 'spread equally among population', unlike savage impact of Tory benefit cuts

DAILY EXPRESS
HOW WILL DYING OF EBOLA AFFECT YOUR PENSION?

DROP DEAD GORGEOUS – PAGE THREE-BOLA STUNNERS INSIDE!!

THE INDEPENDENT
The whole world is running front pages about Ebola. We're not.

Joy In Africa As First White People Get Ebola

by Our West Africa Correspondent
Eppy Demic

THERE were joyous scenes across Africa today as it was confirmed that the first white people in the West had contracted Ebola, meaning a cure would now be on the way.

"For so long the West has looked the other way as thousands of black people have died from Ebola in squalid underfunded clinics," said one doctor in a wretched Sierra Leone hospital overwhelmed with Ebola sufferers.

Don't Know Arse From Ebola

"We could only hope and pray for the day when it would start killing white people in Europe and America and we'd finally get a break."

President Obama said western politicians would now do their best to pretend as if they'd always cared about the epidemic and weren't just throwing money at the problem now as Westerners were sick.

UKIP TRIUMPH

I'm Reckless!

...and I'm legless!

I'm shameless!

Other Top UKIPPERS To Watch As They Take Over Britain This Autumn

1 GRAHAM USELESS, high-flying Euro MP for North Midlands and South Humberside, who could be Ukip's first MP in a Labour seat (or not, if Labour win).

2 KEITH BONELESS, the next Tory MP tipped to join Farage's ever-growing army, if only he can pluck up the courage to defect, which seems unlikely.

3 JEREMY CLUELESS, former Tory local councillor for Market Barkworth, who has become Ukip's chief spokesperson on energy policy and fisheries.

4 MIKE HOPELESS, former Tory parish councillor for Little Barkworth, who came sixth and seventh when he stood for Barking North at the last two general elections, but is now confident that in 2015 it will be third time lucky.

5 GEOFFREY TACTLESS, former Tory supporter, who resigned in protest at "Communist" Cameron's "lurch to the extremist left", and who said on Twitter, "All these black and Asian Poles should be packed off back to Romania, particularly if they are slutty women." *(That's enough, Ed.)*

MP FOR CLACTON

OUT GOES	IN COMES
Tired, moribund MP from party which is hopelessly out-of-touch and has no idea about real people's lives 	Bold, thrusting young MP who's deeply in touch with the concerns of ordinary folks and will shake up those old squares at Westminster 

ST MARY'S THIS SUNDAY: GOD

"Well, thanks again for coming. I was hoping for a bigger turnout, but there we go"

SAYS

Like all its readers, the Sun Is horrified by revelations that the police have been bugging the phones of Sun journalists as they go about their daily life.

Who do these jumped-up coppers think they are – News International?

We'll do the phone hacking, thanks very much, and you stick to arresting our former editors.

ON OTHER PAGES

● Pot Accuses Kettle of Phone Blacking

Those New Hong Kong Ballot Papers In Full

Would you like to be quelled with...

a) Water cannon?
b) Pepper spray?
c) Rubber bullets?
d) Real bullets?
e) Tanks?
f) All of the above?

'Gone Girl' Dissects Modern Marriage

**by Our MeMeMedia Staff
Phillipa Space**

The bestselling book – and now smash hit film – *Gone Girl* dissects modern marriage with a forensic intensity, peeling away the happy veneer and revealing the cynical games couples play.

Who of those amongst us saw that story of Nick and Amy's crumbling relationship, the lies the couple told each other, and the fallout as husband becomes prime suspect in his wife's disappearance, without immediately seeing the grim parallels in one's own marriage?

I know I did, and the results were shocking. Despite checking through all my husband's credit card and phone bills, I could find no evidence that he was cheating on me or planning to murder me. In fact, there was a sense that he was just a nice, decent man doing his best to make me happy.

What chance have I got, trapped in a happy and content marriage like this, of ever writing a viciously cynical bestseller like *Gone Girl*, meaning I wouldn't have to churn out any more lame 5,000-word think pieces about whatever the latest zeitgeisty film is in the cinemas? And for that I put the blame fairly and squarely on my husband for his emotional cruelty, and for not looking like Ben Affleck *(cont. for 5,000 words)*

CAMERON'S CONFERENCE HOWLER
Tory Leader Forgets Deficit

by Our Entire Political Staff
Phil Gallery and **M.T. Hall**

THE POLITICAL world was rocked to its foundations yesterday when David Cameron's keynote speech to the Conservative Party Conference completely overlooked Britain's catastrophic budget deficit.

Speaking without thought, Mr Cameron happily promised lavish tax cuts to millions of voters, completely forgetting that his government is still having to borrow more than £11 billion a month to cover its ever-rising spending commitments.

Said one shocked observer, "I just can't believe that the Prime Minister stood up there talking to us all for an hour and left out any mention of the fact that our national debt has now soared to £1.4 trillion, having doubled since he came to power."

The Acting Leader of the Labour Party, Mr Ed Miliband, was last night quick to launch a savage attack on Mr Cameron's amazing gaffe.

He said, "For one party leader to forget the deficit is forgiveable. For two of them to do so begins to look like unpardonable carelessness."

Mr Miliband then thanked his new scriptwriter, a Mr Oscar Wilde, for coming up with this clever joke, which he had spent days memorising in order to deliver it to the cameras as a brilliant impromptu comment, proving that he does have a sense of humour and is a genuine human being.

Mr Nick Clegg, speaking at the Liberal Democrat Conference, was quick to lash out at what he called "Yet another example of Tory hypocrisy and dishonesty. How anyone could even consider allowing these people to run the country is beyond me."

Observers were quick to note, however, that the Deputy Prime Minister also forgot to mention the deficit run up by his government.

That Labour Front Bench Reshuffle In Full

What you missed in what they are already calling a sea change in British Politics

OUT GOES	IN COMES
Mr Titanic	Mr Iceberg
Mr Rat	Ms Water
Mrs Lifeboat	Mr Fish
Mr Deck Chair	Ms Deck Chair

Mail Online
MP in New Shame

Calls for resignation after Tory backbencher tweets personal bedroom photograph

Here's a picture of my knob
#backbencher

That Graham Norton Line-Up In Full

Graham Naughty: And my guests tonight include, all the way from Australia, the delightful Chardonnay...

(Audience go wild. Naughty takes swig)

...and from Belgium, the one and only Stella Artois...

(Audience go wilder. Naughty has slurp)

...and last but not least, our own Scottish legend, Johnnie Walker...

(Audience goes ballistic. Naughty has glug, then falls off red chair)

© Graham Naughtybutnice.

DEMON CONFESSES TO 'INNER TORIES'

by Our Scandal Staff **Will Selfie**

A MINOR demon yesterday admitted to being tormented by what he called "my inner Conservative MPs". The demon has now resigned from his position after a series of what he described as "shameful errors of judgement".

He said, "I have let down my fellow demons and, above all, my leader Mr Beelzebub. I had everything going for me – a great job, great career prospects on the infernal ladder and, of course, the satisfaction of really helping ordinary people in Hell."

Brookmark of the Beast

He continued, "But my inner Tories encouraged me to take risks and to act in an extreme and out-of-character manner. In a moment of weakness, I exposed myself... as feeble, wet and sad. I am so embarrassed I can only offer my apologies to all my demon colleagues in the Palace of of Pandemonium *(That's enough Paradise Lost. Ed.)*

Life in a UKIP Britain with THE KIPPERS

SIMON WASS

Nursery Times

············ Friday, Once-upon-a-time ············

TOAD AND FRIENDS DRIVEN OUT OF WILD WOOD

By Our Motoring Correspondent **R.G. Bargie**

THE controversial car-loving Mr Toad once again found himself in hot water, after a trip to the Wild Wood in his new car enraged the local weasels and stoats.

Driving with his friends Ratty and Hamster, Mr Toad's car was attacked after the woodland creatures took offence at his number plate "FU WEA5EL5".

Mr Toad was shocked to learn that they interpreted this as in any way abusive. "When I bought this number plate, I had no idea that it would be in any way inflammatory. It's just a pure coincidence," he lied.

The Wild Wood residents found another number plate in the car which read "PI55 0FF 5T0AT5", which Mr Toad explained was another amazing and totally unbelievable coincidence.

The loud-mouthed presenter of Toad Gear told assembled rodents, "There we were, innocently offending everyone – sorry, entertaining everyone – and then we find ourselves subjected to a brutal attack."

The Hamster said, "I'm getting used to this, I've almost died in a car with Mr Toad

once before." Mr Ratty was just ratty. When asked whether he deliberately set out to upset everyone, Mr Toad said, "What a load of Poop-poop."

LATE NEWS

Bake Off goes wrong as finalist's entry runs away

The final of the Great Nurseryland Bake Off ended in chaos today as one of the finalists' signature bakes jumped out of the oven and ran away shouting, "Run, run, as fast as you can, you can't catch me, I'm the Gingerbread Man". He was chased by Mel Pinky and Sue Perky, making innuendos about his "ginger nuts".

On other pages

● Old woman moves from Jimmy Choo Shoe to Clarks Sandal to avoid Mansion Tax **5** ● Sleeping Beauty starts "Wake Up" selfie craze **26** ● Nude pictures of Lady Godiva found in cloud **94**

"Excuse me, can you tell me how to be?"

BRITAIN EXITS AFGHANISTAN

GREEK LAWYERS DEMAND RETURN OF ELGIN MARBLES CASE

by our Human Rights Staff **Geoffrey Rabbitson**

FURIOUS Greek human rights lawyers today petitioned their government for the return of the Elgin Marbles legal case.

Said one enraged Greek legal expert, Kostas Megaloss, "This case has been stolen from us by foreigners. We have been looking after this case for hundreds of years and it was quite safe in our hands.

"But then," he continued, "Mrs Clooney swanned into town, ripped it from us and took the case in triumph back to London to be shown off in her legal firm, Matrix Chambers."

He concluded, "It is an outrage! It is British cultural imperialism at its worst!"

However, a spokesman for Mrs Clooney, a Mr Clooney (played by Danny Ocean), said, "The Greeks had let this case languish for years and it had begun to fall apart with obvious holes in it. It is much better off being looked after by **real** legal experts in Britain who are very careful about handling very valuable old briefs."

Asset frieze

Mr Kostas Megaloss was unimpressed by Mr Clooney's argument, adding, "Large sums of money may have exchanged hands, but that doesn't give them the right to take the priceless Elgin Marbles case away from its natural home."

MONTY PYTHON EXCLUSIVE

Yes! It's the Dead Mother Sketch

(Two men in a bookshop)

John Cleese *(for it is he)*: I wish to register a complaint.

Michael Palin *(for it is also he)*: About a parrot?

John Cleese: No. About my mother.

Michael Palin: Is she resting in peace?

John Cleese: Not if I can help it. This mother is no more! She has ceased to be! She has

shuffled off this mortal coil... Hooray! Now I can put the boot in and sell some books to make enough to pay for all my divorces which are all her fault anyway.

Michael Palin: No, Squire! You want to buy my book instead... beautiful wordage *(continued 2094 Last Ever Money Python Farewell Reunion Tour)*

'Doctors to be paid to do their job' shock

by Our Medical Staff
Dee Mentia and **Al Z. Heimers**

IN A bold new move to drag the NHS into the 21st Century, the government last night announced that it is to pay GPs £55 for spotting that any of their patients are suffering from senile dementia.

Doctors' leaders gave a cautious welcome to the new proposal, but said they hoped it was only the first step in providing suitable incentives to encourage GPs to report many other common complaints.

Speaking from his Algarve holiday home, Dr Ivor Locum said, "Of course this is a good idea, but I now expect the Department of Health to roll out a full 'Monetisation' programme to ensure that millions more patients are drawn into the NHS safety net.

"I suggest that we GPs should receive £150 for identifying anyone with a cold, £200 for spotting a case of 'flu' and £1,000 for correctly diagnosing that the patient is dead".

NEW GP PAYMENT PLAN
How it will work

Doctor: Ah, Mrs Jones, when did you last see a doctor?

Mrs Jones: I can't remember.

Doctor: Excellent! I can now claim my £55. Next patient please...

Everyone at Telegraph Sacked

by **No one**
because they've all been sacked

ONE OF Britain's oldest and most respected newspapers yesterday moved into what its proprietors called "a wholly new era in the development of journalism".

As a first step towards a "complete reinvention" of the traditional newspaper model, the entire staff were served with redundancy notices.

Said the newspaper's Head of Content, Mr R2-D2, based on Planet Tatooine, "We are aiming to become not just a paper-free office but a person-free office, in which our 24/7 rolling digital platform can operate wholly free from any human interference."

He continued, "This article, for instance, is being created entirely electronically, using an algorithm originally developed by software experts employed on Richard Branson's space project."

THE Sun SPECIAL

Dreary's photo casebook
THE FREUD MARRIAGE HAS COMMUNICATION PROBLEMS...

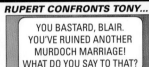

LIZ CONFRONTS MATTHEW...

ADMIT IT... YOU'RE SEEING SOMEONE ELSE

YES, IT'S TONY! I LOVE HIM!

RUPERT CONFRONTS TONY...

YOU BASTARD, BLAIR. YOU'VE RUINED ANOTHER MURDOCH MARRIAGE! WHAT DO YOU SAY TO THAT?

I SAY... DENG DONG! HOW'S THE LOVELY WENDI?

LIZ CONFRONTS MATTHEW AGAIN...

CAN'T YOU SEE HE'S DISLOYAL, SHALLOW, GREEDY, POWER-MAD AND EGOTISTICAL?

I AGREE. YOUR DAD'S A COMPLETE SHIT

COUPLE CONFRONT TRUTH

THAT'S IT... IT'S ALL OVER

ALL OVER THE MAIL AND THE MIRROR, BUT NOT THE SUN, ODDLY...

A message from **Boris Johnson**, Mayor of London

Crikey!

Why's everyone got it in for old Russell Randy? Bojo thinks he's a thoroughly good egg and just because Randy Wandy is jolly funny and a big success with the ladies all the sour-faced lefty killjoys are putting the boot in!

Ok, he's a bit vague on the nitty gritty of policy and a bit of a hypocrite about making oodles of dosh and a bit of a charlatan using lots of long words to bamboozle hoi polloi! Since when was that a crime?!

No, if we started banning ludicrous loquacious lotharios from public life the world would be a lot less colourful!

Which is why, when it comes to the Randy Revolutionary Romeo, I say "Vote for Boris!".

© Mayor of London 2014

---

facebook

Mark Zuckerberg

Still in loving relationship with Her Majesty's Revenue and Customs. Not paying any tax in Britain at all! ☺ LOL ;)

Like . Comment . Share

👍 3

Gary Barlow

Jimmy Carr

Ken Dodd

Share None of my profits

Write a comment...
Bastard

UK Deficit Plummets to New High

by Our Economic Staff **Ban Ki-Rupt**

GEORGE OSBORNE last night announced that the coalition government had succeeded in meeting its number one target of slashing the government deficit from £120 billion to £130 billion per annum.

A delighted chancellor told reporters, "We now have found a way to pay for all the tax-giveaways we are planning before the next election. We will simply borrow the money, and add it to all the other money we've had to borrow.

"Remember, our proudest achievement is that we have delivered on our promise to double the National Debt in five years to a really impressive £1,450,000,000,000. No chancellor in history has ever been able to make such a boast before. And I can promise you, this is only the beginning."

"I think I preferred it when you just had a cigarette afterwards"

mikewilliams.

'WE CAN WIPE OUT LABOUR IN SCOTLAND' Shock New Claim

by Our Scottish Staff **Glen Fiddick**

THE total annihilation of the Scottish Labour Party could become a reality in the next general election according to senior Scottish politicians.

"We can destroy the entire Labour Party north of the border," said a spokeswoman for the Labour Party.

"The referendum has given us the perfect opportunity to eradicate ourselves once and for all and to clear the way for the SNP to take over."

She continued, "This will confound all those critics who say we are ineffectual and do nothing. We are going to attack ourselves full on with an orchestrated campaign of back-biting, disloyalty and self-destruction which will prove once and for all that we are a credible and powerful opposition to the hated Labour Party."

She concluded, "I promise that by the time the election starts we will have ensured that no-one will ever vote again for an untrustworthy group of shallow, self-interested career politicians."

Gordon Brown is 94.

SIR CLIFF TO RAID BBC SHOCK

by Our Legal Staff **Sue Auntie**

THE legendary pop star Sir Clifford Richard last night tipped off the media that he was about to storm into the BBC and remove large amounts of money.

Said a spokesman for the Peter Pan of pop, "Keep it to yourself, but Sir Cliff is going to go in mob-handed with a crack team of hundreds of lawyers and turn the place over. If they find any evidence of cash they will bag it up and take it away."

The BBC criticised Sir Cliff for "overreacting" to what had been, in their opinion, "a low-level armed helicopter assault on a suspected paedophile".

Congratulations and celebrations

Sir Cliff's team rejected the BBC's defence, saying that there were rumours that the BBC headquarters was full of an obscene amount of images featuring the Queen's head and that they were determined to force their way in and retrieve them.

Sir Cliff is 94.

JASON ORANGE LEAVES TAKE THAT

It's a huge loss... so I'll be claiming it against tax

Us too!

Nursery Times

·························· Friday, Once-upon-a-time ··························

FAIRYTALE FARMYARD ROMANCE OVER

By **Beardietricks Rotter**

THEY SAID they would live happily ever after – or at least for a few months – but Nurseryland's golden couple, Jemima Puddleduck and the Fantastic Mr Fux have announced they are to separate.

Farmyard royalty-watchers had said theirs was a match made in Heaven. She the beautiful socialite duck and heir to the Sir Jammy Fishpaste millions, he the priapic predator whose conquests were also in the millions.

They seemed made for each other – she was quackers, he was barking. She was the contributing editor to the New Statesduck and he was a guest columnist for the Guarddog. But friends of Mr Fux (Jeremy Fisher Paxman) tell us that they had arguments about the nature of the paradigm shift necessary for a cultural revolution in the barn and very soon the foxy side of Mr Fux began to show itself.

The couple have not been seen in public together and top tweeter, Jenny Wren, has revealed that they've unfollowed each other on Twitter. So, the split looks final.

Ms Puddleduck's former farmyard beaux have included Imrani Cricket, the dashing insect turned politician, and Hugh Grunt, the celebrity swine and supporter of the campaign for cider press regulation, Applejacked Off. *(Yes, we get the idea. Ed.)*

 Dave Snooty AND HIS NO PALS

NO-ONE LIKES DAVE SNOOTY...

OH NO! I'M SNOBBY NO MATES!

WHAT CAN I DO TO BE MORE POPULAR?

GET LOST! HAW! HAW!

BUT DAVE HAS A BRILLIANT IDEA...

HERE'S 20 REASONS WHY YOU SHOULD BE MY PAL

WE'RE QUIDS IN WITH DAVE!

WHAT A GIVEAWAY!

YES - IT SHOWS HE'S DESPERATE!

IF YOU THINK YOU CAN BRIBE ME... YOU'RE NOT VERY MUCH MISTAKEN!

HOORAH FOR BOOTY - I MEAN SNOOTY!

IT'S A **BUY** ELECTION, EH, READERS!?!

SCOTLAND LARD

FAT POLICE SHOCK ==

ROBERT THOMPSON

Feminist T-shirt Sweat Shop Scandal
A NATION REACTS

Daily Mail

62P AN HOUR IS A DISGRACE – THEY SHOULD BE PAID HALF THAT

theguardian

62p an hour is a disgrace – why can't they get interns to do it for free?

The Sun

THE T-SHIRTS ARE A DISGRACE – WHY AREN'T THEY WET?

★ Morning Star

THE T-SHIRTS ARE A DISGRACE – they should read 'This is what a Leninist looks like'

DAILY EXPRESS

HURRAH FOR THE SWEAT SHOPS! AT LEAST THE FOREIGN WORKERS AREN'T OVER HERE

The Daily Telegraph

Why Isn't Fruity But Pregnant Kate Wearing the T-Shirt?

London Evening Standard

Evgeny Lebedev Shows Us HIS T-Shirt In An Exclusive Photo-Shoot

THE TIMES

Caitlin Moran recalls the t-shirts of her youth

BuzzFeed The Top Ten Sweat Shop T-shirts...

1. 'This is what an opportunist looks like', 2. 'This is what a capitalist looks like', 3. 'This is what a Faragist looks like', 4. 'This is what a naturist looks like' *(a tattoo, obviously, rather than a t-shirt!)* 5. 'This is what a list looks like', etc

---

Alas Jones and Jones

UK OLD 4.17amv

Griff 1: I mean, if I have to pay this mansion tax, I'm going to leave the country.

Griff 2: What? And live in the town?

Griff 1: Naaaa. I've got a great big house in the town and a great big house in the country.

Griff 2: Which country's that, Griff? Whichever one you've got your yacht in?

Griff 1: Naaaa. This one. Britain. If the Labour party, under that Ed Mili... Mili... Mili...

Griff 2: Millionaire?

Griff 1: No, that's me.

Griff 2: Miliband!

Griff 1: That's the one. Anyway, if Miliband brings in this mansion tax thingy, it'll cost me a fortune.

Griff 2: But you've got a fortune, haven't you, Griff?

Griff 1: Yeah, but I mean, you're talking thousands and thousands of pounds.

Griff 2: What, your fortune?

Griff 1: No, that's millions. The tax is thousands.

Griff 2: So you can pay it without much trouble?

Griff 1: Yeah, well, I can pay it, but it's the principle, isn't it?

Griff 2: What's that then, Griff?

Griff 1: Because to earn the money to pay the bill I'll have to go back on telly. And no one wants that.

Griff 2: Or you could go back and play Fagin in Oliver.

Griff 1: Oh yeah.

Both Griffs sing: 'In this life one thing counts, in the bank, large amounts.'

(Laughter and applause at classic Pete and Dud two-hander)

TWITTER HATE STORM

by Our Media Correspondent

IN A growing off-line row, millions of people today agreed how much they hate Twitter with its endless toxic stupidity and its *(cont. p94)*

Theresa May
Desert Island Discs Highlights

Kirsty Youngperson: Home Secretary, will you be lonely on your desert island?

Theresa May: No, because I would expect a huge influx of people coming onto my desert island by boat, raft, swimming etc, and I won't be able to stop them, so there will be thousands of us and I'll have plenty of company.

Kirsty Youngperson: So what's your next record?

Theresa May: It's got to be Record Number of Immigrants. *(Continued 94kHz)*

"Uh, oh, looks like we're toast"

MILIBAND DOWN AND OUT

How much change do you want?

Well I'd prefer Alan Johnson, but I'd settle for Yvette Cooper

MIKE READ CALYPSO DISGRACE

by Our Pop Music Staff **Carrie Bean**

TOP 70s entertainment stars were last night attempting to distance themselves from top 70s entertainment star Mike Read, after the revelation that he'd been involved in a shameful Calypso incident, dating back to last week.

Policeman investigating Operation Yew Kip found that Mike Read was guilty of inappropriate singing with over-aged members of the public. Video evidence of Read's shocking behaviour is now on Yew Tube, where he can clearly be seen with his hands on a guitar whilst uttering unspeakable things.

The Hairy Cornflake, DLT, speaking from his solicitors' office, said, "Read's behaviour is inexcusable, and gives a bad name to being a Seventies entertainment star. I know that times are different nowadays, but it's no excuse to get into bed with Ukip."

Rolf Harris, speaking from his prison cell, said "comedy songs have never been funny, as I proved many times. And one about Ukip?! You've got to be pulling my extra leg, diddle, diddle, diddle, dum."

The late Jimmy Savile, speaking from beyond the grave, said, "This appalling lapse of taste is... *(Okay, we get the idea, Ed.)*

Another couple of pints and I'll do a collapso!

"Kids today! What do they know?"

Nursery Times

.... Friday, Once-upon-a-time ....

TROLL TO GET TWO-YEAR SENTENCE

By Our Social Media Staff **Tweetie Pie**

A TROLL caught harassing three members of the Billy Goat Gruff family from underneath a bridge yesterday protested at the severity of his sentence.

"It was just banter," said the troll. "My messages were misconstrued and I was clearly joking when I threatened to eat them all."

But the largest of the Billy Goat Gruff family said, "The troll carried out a systematic campaign of abuse. He started by calling us fat because we were enjoying eating the grass, then he criticised us for going trip-trap over what he claimed was his bridge and then finally he threatened to gobble us all up and crush us to bits, body and bone."

Defenders of the troll said that putting a poor, ugly creature in jail for a few "robust and colourful" exchanges with the Billy Goat community was an attack on free speech and an attempt to stifle valid criticism of public bovine behaviour.

Said one troll sympathiser, "Really, this goat and his kids should stop bleating and develop a thicker skin – that would certainly make them tastier when we eat them. Only joking! Has everyone lost their sense of humour?"

The Billy Goats Gruff claimed that the two-year sentence was a triumph for the Nurseryland judicial system.

"One should be able," said the youngest one, "to put one's head above the parapet of the bridge without it being bitten off."

Should Woolf be in charge of inquiry?

Questions were asked in the Nurseryland Parliament about the suitability of Fiona Woolf to look into historic allegations of wolves abusing little pigs.

Suggestions were made that as a Woolf, who had regularly enjoyed drinks with other big bad wolves, she was bound to let off any establishment wolves implicated in crimes against piglets. Mrs Woolf said, "I'm sure this will all blow over, when I huff and puff." However, a pig in a brick house warned, "This Woolf could end up in hot water."

KISS OF DEATH ENDORSEMENT

"You're all right!"

"Oh, fuck!"

Wilfred Owen arrested by Operation Yewtree

by Our Historic Crime Staff
Nicholas Witchunt

THE late First World War poet Wilfred Owen is the latest celebrity to come to the attention of the police after the Mail on Sunday revealed disturbing allegations that he was "a cowardly paedo who should be shot".

The Mail on Sunday has warned schoolchildren not to read his poetry for fear that they will be exposed to his creepy anti-war sentiments and will be groomed as pacifists and *(cont. p94)*

"Yes, you're dead, but in a good way"

THOSE VICTORIOUS REPUBLICANS IN FULL

Mitt Looney, 39 A wealthy businessman who campaigned on cancelling Obamacare and legislating for citizens' "inalienable right" to fire guns inside schools whenever they feel it is necessary.

Wackey Ernst, 45 An ex-pig castrator from Iowa who campaigned on a platform of cutting off Democrats' testicles and selling them in order to lower America's national debt, as well as cancelling Obamacare.

George F. Bush, 23 The "F" in Bush Junior's name stand for "Fucking-Yet-Another", but don't let that fool you – he is very much his own man! He believes in repealing Obamacare, increasing tax breaks for enormous corporations and a third Gulf War to "finally sort the whole region right out".

Crazy Bob Ruskitt, 58 A traditional Republican, Ruskitt wants to repeal Obamacare, legally declare gay marriage an "unholy abomination in the eyes of Jehovah" and establish the death penalty for recycling.

Mia Barking, 38 First black Republican Congresswoman. Very keen on bills encouraging turkeys to vote for Christmas, sawing Mexico off the bottom of America and repealing Obamacare.

Sheeza Saico, 14 A real prodigy, newly-elected lawmaker Saico's radical policies include compulsory 4X4 cars for the under-12s, the first ever pledge to lower the abortion cut-off point to six hours, and the repeal of Obamacare.

(That's enough victorious Republicans. Ed.)

APPLE BOSS COMES OUT

by Our Silicon Valley Staff **Gay Lord**

TIM Cook, the CEO of Apple, this week shocked the world by publicly declaring himself to be a "tax avoider, and proud of it".

Mr Cook said that for too long he had been reluctant to admit that he preferred not paying tax, because there was still a stigma in some blinkered societies attached to failing to pay your fair share to the public purse.

"I hope this opens the door for other high-profile American company bosses to admit that they too are openly not paying any UK tax, and that this should be a source of pride, not embarrassment."

He continued, "Beforehand, I felt that I was living a lie, but now I don't mind being seen in public with my accountant and admitting that we're in a very happy and highly profitable relationship."

US midterms: Obama vows to carry on getting nothing done

by Our Man in Washington
Jim Naughtiebutnice

Barack Obama has sworn that the Democratic Party's setbacks in the US midterm elections will not hold him back from his long-term plan to achieve almost nothing during his eight years in government.

"I hope, and know that you hope, and I know that you hope I hope," he wearily told a crowd of his few remaining supporters, "that these results will not hinder or impede my progress towards the proud goal of total gridlock, which we started six whole years ago.

"I have a dream," he went on, "that eventually Republicans and Democrats will agree on one thing, ie that they both hate me and will be so busy fighting that nobody can ever do anything again except play golf."

Who should replace Lady Woolf, the outgoing Lord Mayor of London, as chair of the independent historic abuse inquiry? You decide...

Top lawyer Mrs Clooney

Top Judge John Deed

Top Judge Len Goodman

Top Judge Cheryl Fernandez-Versini

Top civil servant Sir John Chilcot

Top pop star Gary Glitter

Top politician Lord Brittan QC

Fiona Woolf again

UKIP IN DRIVING SEAT

"Where to, Guv?"

"1957 – and step on it!"

THAT MARK RECKLESS VICTORY SPEECH IN FULL

"WE in Ukip are the heirs to the great radical tradition in British politics. Ukip is in a long line of reformers and rebels which includes the Levellers, the Chartists, the Suffragettes, the Borrowers, the Ramblers, the Tolpuddle Martyrs, the Birmingham 6, the cast of Made in Dagenham, the Beatles, the Pre-Raphaelites, the SWP, the Cumberbitches and, of course, the Monster Raving Loony Party *(Is this right? Ed.)*."

"Does my bum look big enough in this?"

Controversial picture of enormous arse provokes debate

by **Kim Kardashian**

ONE HAS to go back to the appearance of the original Hottentot Venus in the London drawing room of the Duchess of Bury in 1830, to discover a bigger arse than that pictured last week.

The picture of the arse *(see above)*, came from America and has appeared in numerous television shows and in all the papers. What does it say about society when so many people are just staring at this massive arse with their mouths open in a state of utter incomprehension?

Is this arse a statement about empowerment or is it an embarrassing condemnation of our lack of values, and moral turpitude? Who cares – let's just have another look at the arse on Mail Online, where it is now contributing editor.

The Nigel Farage *Bayeux Tapestry Tie*

THE tie that says it all about ghastly foreigners coming over here and ruining the country with their appalling Norman language, architecture, food, administrative system, judicial framework and cultural sophistication due to their links with mainstream Europe which enabled England to develop into a country that dominated... hang on... (That's enough. Ed.)

The Ukip Revolution NEW-LOOK BRITAIN

OUT GO
Middle-class, middle-aged, white, male, public school Tories

IN COME
The true voice of the real people of Britain in the shape of, er... middle-class, middle-aged, white (er...)

Boris in air rage incident

by Our Aviation Staff **Amy Johnson**

The Mayor of London was this week involved in a dramatic fight aboard a passenger jet flying back from Malaysia. Trouble began when one of the passengers, a Mr Johnson, began insisting that the plane land not at Heathrow, but in the middle of the Thames Estuary on what he called "Boris Island".

As passengers tried to calm him down, Boris continued to argue the case for a third London airport, and objected when he had to be restrained by stewards, saying, "Get off, I want to be restrained by stewardesses. Where are the fruity trolley dollies?! Ding dong."

Eventually the Mayor was handcuffed, at his insistence, to a First Class reclining seat. Luckily, another passenger then went mad, taking away all the attention. When asked if drink was involved, members of the Mayor's team said, "No – Boris is always like that."

THE KIPPERS SIMON WASS

No offence, but Britain's being flooded!

...moving in and taking over the country...

You're right, the numbers are terrifying...

Yes... bloody Ukippers!!

The Secret DIARY OF SIR JOHN MAJOR KG aged 77¾

Monday

I was not inconsiderably surprised to turn on the television, whilst eating my favourite breakfast cereal "Golden Greyones", to find a familiar figure on the screen, dressed up in jungle gear and standing near a spider. "What are you watching?" asked my wife, Norman, "and what's that poisonous creature doing?"

"I have no idea," I said. "It's Edwina Currie having a shower," she replied. "Oh, is it? I had no idea. But it is, in my judgement, of no interest," I said. "Then why are your glasses all steamed up?" she asked, unhelpfully. "You're not in the jungle, why are you all hot and bothered?"

At this point I suggested that we should stop this argument and I should turn over to a news channel, to continue my research into public views on the question of immigration.

"I am writing a not altogether unimportant speech about European border controls," I said. "Allow me to help," she said, "I can think of at least one person who shouldn't be allowed back into the country, and whose freedom of movement should be restricted to a tank full of scorpions in the Australian Bush for ever."

"And who is that?" I enquired innocently. But instead of answering she accidentally tipped the bowl of soggy wheat squares all over my head, which did at least remove the steam from my spectacles. Oh yes.

"Oh, hi, is Dave in?"

Sheffield unites against disgraced former star

MORE signatories have joined the campaign to try to stop former Lib Dem star Nick Clegg from representing Sheffield ever again. "He has shown no remorse even though he's obviously guilty," said one angry local. "He knew what he was doing when he got into bed with a complete stranger."

One supporter disagreed, saying, "He's served his full term, I don't see the problem."

However, most agreed that he should never be allowed anywhere near a ballot box again. "It's a disgrace – he's supposed to be a role model," said local footballer Ched Evans.

Fruity woman who had affair with man who then had affair with another woman comes over to sell book

by **Phil Page**

A HUGE picture of a fruity French woman in a dress split to the thigh today flew onto the front page of this newspaper. Some readers expected there to be a story about her inside, but there wasn't because it is too boring and we've read it all before.

INSIDE
- Pics of fruity Dame Helen Mirren in bikini **p3**
- Huge pic of fruity Myleene Klass **p4**
- Pic of Benedict Cumberbatch's fruity fiancée, the "Mrs Sherlock-to-be" *(surely the "Mrs Alan Turing-to-be"?)* **p6**

PLUS pic of fruity Gillian Anderson showing cleavage on TV.

PLUS some news (but not much, to be honest)

It's all in your super, sexy, phwoaraway KissandTellegraph!!!

STONEHENGE TUNNEL SCHEME 'NOT NEW' SAY EXPERTS

by Our Transport Staff **Cecil Roads**

THE Government's new plans to spend £2 billion on a two-mile-long road tunnel underneath Stonehenge are only the latest in a long line of similar plans down the millennia, none of which has yet come to fruition.

"It was not long after the erection of Stonehenge in the Neolithic Age," says Professor Mary Beard, "that our Bronze Age ancestors were already talking about the need for a tunnel to keep traffic away from this sacred astronomical observatory (or possibly burial site, or whatever it is)."

When the Romans arrived, they revived the plan for a Stonehenge by-pass, as part of their 20-billion-sestertii road-building programme covering the whole of Britain.

However, once they had completed the Fosse Way, Ermine Street and the rest of their chariot-based infrastructure, they found they had no money left for the "Stonehenge fly-under", as it was known.

In Norman times, William Rufus was keen to resuscitate the Roman plan for Stonehenge, but an environmental protestor of the time, William "de Swampy" Tyrrell, shot him through the eye and the plans had once again to be shelved.

Of all the many plans which followed over the centuries, the most ambitious of all was that of Isambard Kingdom Brunel, who planned an enormous 20-mile-long aqueduct along which giant, steam-driven ships could carry millions of Victorian tourists to gaze at what has now become our most revered World Heritage site.

But Brunel's visionary project was never *(cont. p94)*

EU's Juncker tells Cameron: 'Obey the rules or get out'

by Our Brussels Staff
Polly Pot and Martin Kettle

The president of the European Commission, Mr Jean-Claude Junckbond, today warned David Cameron that he had "no chance whatsoever" of getting the EU to change its rules on "freedom of movement or anything else".

Said Mr Junckmail, "In the EU, the accepted procedure is that everybody obeys the rules – except for, of course, myself."

He explained, "The fact that I was in charge of a gigantic and illegal tax scam in Luxembourg, which openly defied all the relevant principles on which the EU was founded, may on the face of it seem contradictory.

"But I have set up a top-level inquiry to look into it all, which will be chaired by no less a figure than the president of the European Commission.

"Without giving anything away at this stage," Mr Juncketing concluded, "I can assure you that my inquiry will find that everything I did was entirely above board and in keeping with the guiding spirit of the EU.

"My actions over these tax arrangements were not taken in any way to promote a narrow, petty, national interest – unlike the outrageous suggestion of Mr Cameron that the rules should be bent to serve the interests of his own ridiculous little country."

"Blimey, Olivia Colman REALLY is in everything!"

Enormous Political Metaphor Runs Aground

by Our Political Staff
Phil Paper

A huge symbol of the state of the political parties in Britain was last night beached on the comment pages of all Britain's national newspapers.

The image of a ship listing on one side and being washed up on the rocks was just too tempting for political analysts, sketch writers and cartoonists.

"We couldn't avoid it," said one editor. "No matter how hard we tried to steer away, we ended up stuck with the same vast metaphor as everyone else."

Salvage experts calculate that the metaphor representing either the Tory/Lib Dem/Labour party *(delete as applicable)* is likely to take weeks to shift, but there are fears that the figurative icon of a ship that has lost its sense of direction and been forced to run aground onto shifting sands with rats leaving it could still be there right up to May. *(That's enough political metaphor. Ed.)*

Eye TV Review

The Missing
Gloomy, upsetting drama in which James Nesbitt tries to find out what's happened to a missing child.

The Fall
Downbeat, gritty crime series in which a glum Gillian Anderson tries to catch a miserable serial killer.

The Broadchurch
Olivia Colman and David Tennant look sad in this sad series about yet more murdered children being murdered, by a murderer.

The Repeat
Violent, disquieting series in which lots of murders... hang on, hasn't this exact series just been on under another name?

The Killing
Sarah Lund returns in a gritty, miserable series, where her task is to find out exactly who has stolen the blueprint of her original show and tortured it for the last seven years.

Who should be the next mayor of London? You choose!

| Diane Abbott | Jeremy Paxman | Russell Brand | Edwina Currie | Prince George | Alan Johnson | Dr Johnson | Boris Johnson (again) |

THE ☰ TIMES

19 December 2014

CIA torture revelations – why it wouldn't happen here…

Because we wouldn't reveal any of it.

George W. Bush 'denies knowledge'

by Our Torture Correspondent **Walter Bording**

In the wake of the damning CIA torture report regarding the post 9/11 events, George W Bush has denied having any knowledge of being president.

"I remember sitting in the Oval Office playing cards with the security guards, watching Jack Bauer kill the baddies on *24*

and hiding whenever Old Man Grumpy Pants Cheney came in, but I sure as shucks don't remember being president," the former president told reporters.

"I'm sure if I had been president for eight years someone would have mentioned it to me.

"Like the detainees, I was kept totally in the dark and occasionally given a glass of water."

That leaked James Bond movie script
– redacted version (not in full…)

INTERIOR: DUNGEON. NIGHT

(The door opens. A British secret agent enters.)

Agent: The name's ▮▮▮▮ , James ▮▮▮▮ .

CIA Agent: Hello, Mr Bond, I've been expecting you. Have you come to take part in this interrogation?

Bond: No, Felix, I have no idea who you are or what's going on.

Felix Leiter: Well, it's obvious. I'm water ▮▮▮▮ ing this terrorist suspect.

Bond: So he'll be shaken AND stirred!

Felix Leiter: And after that I'll be giving him a hummus ▮▮▮▮ up the ▮▮▮▮ .

Bond: That should get to the bottom of it!

Felix Leiter: Same old British humour! Good thing you're not here to make light of the issue.

Bond: Do you expect him to talk?

Felix Leiter: No, Mr ▮▮▮▮ , I expect him to die.

Bond: Isn't that against the ▮▮▮▮ Convention?

Felix Leiter: No. I've got a licence to ▮▮▮▮ . You got a problem with that, James?

Bond: No, that's fine. So long as I don't know about it. What's the suspect revealed so far?

Felix Leiter: I'm afraid I can't tell you.

Bond: Why, is it top secret?

Felix Leiter: No, he just hasn't told us anything.

Miss Money ▮▮▮▮ enters.

Miss ▮▮▮▮ penny: James! British Foreign Secretary ▮▮▮▮ Straw wants to talk to you.

Bond: But I'm not here.

▮▮▮▮ Moneypenny: He knows that!

(Enter Bond girls, Torture Galore, Plenty O'Violence and Solitaire Confinement, wearing orange bikini jumpsuits and dancing to hit Bond theme song "Lie and Let Die").

© The For Your Eyes Sony Corporation, 2014

ELGIN MARBLES LENT TO RUSSIA

Nice art!

MARBLES MAN SAYS 'WE WON'T GIVE THEM BACK'

by Our Archaeological Staff **Nick Stuff**

A HUGE international storm erupted yesterday as the figure at the centre of the latest diplomatic row declared that he would not return the disputed treasures of the Crimea and Eastern Ukraine.

Mr Putin, the Russian curator who is widely believed to have lost his marbles, said, "I am keeping these marvellous historical jewels because I do not believe they would be safe in the hands of their owners."

He continued, "They just won't look after them properly there, whereas we Russians will guard them carefully with our expert

tanks and armed personnel."

The aggrieved local authorities have launched a formal protest with the United Nations and are hoping that Mrs Clooney will take up their cause.

"We know Amal is really busy with important human rights issues like statues from a 2,000-year-old frieze, but perhaps her well-informed husband could intercede."

George Clooney issued a statement calling on Vladimir Rasputin to give the UK back to the Crimea and to tell the Earl of Balaclava to withdraw the Light Brigade from the Pantheon.

"Darling, look… a full moon"

25

DIARY

VALERIE TRIERWEILER

I have always been a very, very sensitive woman. I cannot hear a child cry without blocking my ears. Nor can I see an old woman begging for money without crossing the street. And if anyone ever knocks on my office door for advice, I let them have it.

Call it female intuition, call it what you will, but I felt a subtle change in François Hollande's attitude to me from the moment he was first elected President.

Was it his suggestion that, all in all, it might be more convenient for me to live in London? Or was it his way of holding his nose whenever I entered the room? Or perhaps it was his new habit of putting on a suit, a tie and a motorcycle helmet every time he got dressed.

How could I forget those first few years of passion with François? That once-in-a-lifetime passion that devours everything.

I was a young journalist, so wide-eyed and unworldly that I was still barely on my second marriage. He was the proud standard-bearer of the Left, passionate about equality, liberty and fraternity, but whose life had taken a tragic turn for the worse after he had unwittingly fathered four children by the cold, haughty Ségolène Royal.

So concerned was he with the poor and the oppressed that he realised too late that he had been trapped in a loveless union for the past fifteen years.

It all started so innocently. Our friendship was purely professional. It was a hot summer's day when I asked François to my apartment to discuss climate change.

Passionate about energy conservation, I had long considered it my duty as a concerned citizen to save on air-conditioning by removing my clothes.

I would never have imagined that François would react in the way that he did. With his razor-sharp intellect, he immediately comprehended the logic of my stance and hastily removed his clothes too.

"But shall I keep my motorcycle helmet on?" he whispered softly in my ear.

"Yes, François," I said. "But turn it the other way round. You look so much better that way."

As our relationship progressed, my heart soared on an ocean of joy, leaping up and down in my mouth like a beautiful white dove ready to explode with happiness.

NEW 'OLDER' BOND GIRL

Dear friends tell me I am too thoughtful for my own good. Despite what Ségolène Royal may have you believe, I always treated that horse-faced harridan with the most perfect grace.

It was François for whom I felt sorry. How had he let himself be duped by this cold-hearted frump into having four children and staying shackled to her for 29 years?

When François and I first moved into the Elysée Palace, I was determined never to lose sight of our Socialist principles. For this reason, I moved François' office into the smaller, more egalitarian rooms at the back. "You are now truly a man of the people, François!" I exclaimed as he squeezed into his cosy cubby-hole.

It was only then that I realised that something would have to be done with the large space we had just vacated. After much debate, I thought it best to move my own office in there. But it was clearly absurd for one woman and two secretaries to occupy such a vast area. With this in mind, and to help set an example in our drive for full employment, and to help in our fight for women in our society, I hired four more secretaries, a professional dresser and a couple of press advisers.

Needless to say, the media wilfully misunderstood my intentions. I was literally struck in the face by a tsunami of fireworks borne aloft on a roaring herd of vipers. Such is the fate of the progressive feminist in our society, her only thought being for the welfare of others less accomplished than herself!

Amidst this fiery avalanche of spears and arrows, I thought I could count on the support of François. How wrong I was! Instead, he kept insisting he needed to attend to urgent business, and always in that same motorcycle helmet. He insisted it was for added protection, in the event of a crash. I thought nothing of it at the time. It was only later that it struck me as unusual for a President to wear a helmet while being chauffeur-driven in the official limousine.

The hammer-blow came when I heard a newspaper was planning to print photographs of François walking out of the home of an actress wearing only his helmet. It was as though a hornets' nest had opened up to flatten me.

At first he denied it. He claimed it had nothing to do with him: he said his helmet often went out in the evening on its own.

Something made me think he was not telling the truth. I pressed him further. He confessed, saying that he couldn't take my histrionics any more. What do you mean – my histrionics? "How dare you – you bald bastard!" I screamed, pulling his shirt off, feeding it into the food mixer and setting the dial to Fast Mince before locking myself in the bathroom, curling up on the cold tiles and feeding myself with as many pills as I could. No one calls me histrionic and gets away with it.

Seventy-eight. I counted them. He sent me 78 text messages yesterday. And 83 the day before. And tomorrow he'll send me a further 92. How do I know this? Because I write them for him. You see, I am a woman, and only a woman knows the secrets of a man's heart. François is obsessed by me. He realises he will never be a great President without Valérie Trierweiler by his side, looking beautiful in her wedding dress. I have always been a very, very sensitive woman; if he does not know this already, he certainly will once I've finished with him.

As told to
CRAIG BROWN

Forgotten Moments In Music History

Not much call for seating at Ben E King's funeral

Nancy took a while to work out what her boots were made for

In fairness, the people of the town weren't entirely wrong

Farage defends new Ukip candidate for Essex seat

by Our Political Staff **Peter O'Bore**

UKIP LEADER Nigel Farage today gave his 100 percent backing to his party's latest choice to fight the key Essex marginal of Basilbrush.

Mr Kevin Barrelscrape is the 94th prospective candidate adopted for the seat in the past 93 days, following a succession of embarrassments when, one after another, each of the previous candidates was discovered to be either a serial fantasist, a closet racist, a committed homophobe or an inveterate fiddler of his expenses.

Said Mr Farage to thousands of waiting newsmen, "I am right behind Mr Barrelscrape, who tells me he has a double first in nuclear physics from Oxford College, Cambridge, that many of his best friends are 'Chinky Poos' and 'Pooftahs', and that it is at least 10 years since he did time for accounting irregularities."

Shortly after Mr Barrelscrape had been formerly adopted by the 23 remaining Ukip members in Basilbrush, he was forced to stand down when it was discovered that he was an illegal immigrant whose real name is Vladislav Barrolscrapskii and who had come over to England in the hope of taking someone's job as a Ukip candidate.

GARGLEBOX

Tonight, Steph and Dom from Gogglebox are sitting on the sofa, watching "Steph and Dom Meet Nigel Farage" on television...

STEPH: Who the hell are they?

DOM *(pouring huge refill of whisky)***:** I think they're called Geoff and Tom.

STEPH: And who's the drunk one?

DOM: Well, they *all* are, darling.

STEPH: No, the really drunk one who's making an arse of himself...

DOM: It's that UKIP chap. I think he's called Fararse.

STEPH: Oh yes, Nigel Fararse! What's he doing on a silly show like that?

DOM: Getting smashed by the looks of it.

STEPH: Like his glass!

DOM: Very good, darling.

STEPH: And why is he talking about testicles?

DOM: Because the whole programme's balls.

STEPH: Brilliant, darling! *We* should be on that show!

DOM: What, being filmed just getting pissed? Sounds like a terrible idea.

BOTH: Hahahahahahahaha!

(He tops up both their drinks)

Old Etonian actor takes US by storm

by Our Showbiz Staff
Oscar Wildeabouttheboy

Following in the footsteps of Hugh Laurie, Dominic West and Damian Lewis, the latest Old Etonian to wow the US audience is posh super-smoothie David Cameron.

Tory of Everything

Cameron was given the red-carpet treatment by admiring American fans, who hailed his performance as a man who overcomes severe disabilities to triumph as a world famous prime minister as "astonishing".

Said one critic, Mr B. Obama, "David can play any part he likes. He is a genius. I would go so far as to say that he is the greatest British actor since Tony Blair.

"David can do tough, sensitive, funny, sad and – of course – deferential, which I like very much. It's only when he tries an American accent that he fails to convince."

Mr Cameron replied, "Yo, Brobama, wazzup dude?"

'Interstellar' Filmgoers Complain of Audio Quality

by Our Film Critic
Kate Mumble

EVEN though Christopher Nolan's sci-fi blockbuster looks set to break box office records, thousands of cinema fans have been asking for their money back on account of "problems with the sound".

Said one, "We could hear every word perfectly, as the terrible dialogue poured out of the wooden actors – not a single syllable was lost."

Said another, "I wish I'd bought some popcorn to drown out the sound. Lines like 'love transcends the limits of time and space' and 'our destiny lies above us' were all too audible – even above the retching noises of the audience."

The director, however, urged viewers not to give away the time-travelling movie's big plot twist – that you feel like you age 100 years whilst you're watching it.

POETRY CORNER

**In Memoriam
Deborah Devonshire
1920-2014**

So. Farewell
Then "Debo", the
Dowager Duchess of
Devonshire.

Now you have
Died. But is that
In real life or on
Downton Abbey?

A beautiful aristocrat
With lots of sisters,
The original "It girl"
Who danced with the
American President,
Had tea with Hitler
And married a Duke.

It's all so
Preposterous, it
Can only have
Been written by
Julian Fellowes.

E.J. Thribb
(17½ ad breaks)

Who will be the new editor of the Guardian? You decide...

Janine Gibson

Ian Katz

Kath Viner

Unpaid intern

Richard Ingrams

Harry Potter

Still Alan Rusbridger, basically

27

guardian SPECIAL

Why those Christmas songs are patronising and wrong

By Holly Toynbee

Do They Know It's Christmas? – yes, of course they do, since there are 500 million Christians in Africa.

White Christmas – what's wrong with a black one? They have Christmas in Africa too, you know?

O Little Town of Bethlehem – no, it isn't, it's quite a big town actually and it doesn't lie still because it's occupied by the Israelis, thank you very much.

We Three Kings of Orient Are – are you? Where are the Queens then, stuck at home, while you're out with your mates, following stars?

The 12 Days of Christmas – no, there aren't, there are 50 at least, now that Christmas has become a consumer festival starting as soon as the shops have finished with Hallowe'en.

Good King Wenceslas – no, he wasn't. What sort of country consigns its old-age peasants to spending the Feast of Stephen collecting their own fuel?

I Wish It Could Be Christmas Everyday – oh thanks, Wizzard, what about Diwali and Eid and Hanukkah? No room for them on the calendar, apparently? Typical.

Mistletoe and Wine – well, that's just an incitement to sexual harassment. Why not throw in rohypnol while you're about it, Sir Cliff?

Wonderful Christmastime – no, it isn't, Sir Paul. The world's a very unhappy place – as you'd know if you listened to all the charity singles that are out at this time of year. Honestly.

© the Groaniad 2014

Comedy	Tragedy	Facelift

Royston

Pick of the Pantos

IF it's laughs you want, head on down to the Octagon in Swindon where there's a hilarious Dick Whittington.

TV historian Dr Lucy Worsley is in thigh-slapping form as Dick, ably assisted by TV's Michael Buerk as King Rat, TV's Jeremy Paxman as Dame Wishy-Washy, TV's Judy Murray as Aladdin and a surprise appearance by TV's Alan Johnson as Postman Pat.

★ **Eye rating:** *Their career's behind them!*

THOSE CHRISTMAS TANK TOPS IN FULL

Little George

Little Vlad

POETRY CORNER

In Memoriam Mandy Rice-Davies, leading character in the Profumo affair of the 1960s

So. Farewell
Then Mandy Rice-Davies,
Good time girl,
Nightclub owner,
Part-time actress and
Good friend of
Mrs Thatcher.

If you knew that
Private Eye's official
Threnodist had
Written a poem
About your life,
Doubtless you'd
Say, "He would,
Wouldn't he?"

E.J. Thribb (17½)

TONIGHT'S TV

That Mitchell and Pleb Look

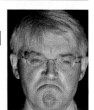

HOW TO AVOID CANCER

1. Be lucky

2. Don't smoke

3. But mainly be lucky

4. Er... that's it

5. Good luck.

GNOME MART

Letters to the Editor

Why, oh why, must James Bond now be black?

SIR – Recent weeks have seen speculation that the actor Idris Elba might be selected to play the next James Bond. As various commentators have correctly pointed out, it is simply ridiculous to suggest that James Bond could be played by a black man. In Fleming's books it is quite clear that Bond is a Scottish milkman called Sean *(Rough Diamonds Are Forever, p94)*.

To recast Bond as a member of an ethnic minority is quite simply unrealistic and I suggest the producers forget about such fanciful politically correct gimmicks and return to the stark realism of the early Bond films, in which Bond nearly has his genitals cut off by a laser, or turns a car into a plane, or goes to space, or uses an ejector seat to throw villains from his Aston Martin, or defuses a nuclear bomb in thirty seconds, or has an invisible car, or arrives on a beach with a tuxedo on under his wetsuit, or defeats an entire base of heavily armed men, armed with nothing more than a pencil. To turn Bond into a black man completely defeats the hard work the filmmakers have done to make him a plausible, nuanced and three-dimensional character.
Sir Herbert Gusset
The Old Asylum,
Loonraker, Somerset.

An Open Letter from Tony Blair to Ed Miliband

Look, no one supports you, Ed, more than I do. But, hey, you've got some work to do if you want to get elected. Because what people want, Ed, is a Labour party that's not stuck in the left-wing past. A sort of "New Labour". And what people want from a leader is not someone who is young and goofy, and can't eat a bacon sandwich, but someone older, more tanned, with better teeth and a great butt (thanks, Wendy!).

I dunno, I think cool Britannia wants someone who is not afraid to take on the unions, embrace big business, invade Iraq, sanction waterboarding, build up a property portfolio, manage a consultancy empire, suck up to the world's most unpleasant dictators...

I don't know where you would find this kind of guy, Ed, but if I can help you in any way then you know my number... it's £500,000 per hour!

Yours, Tony Blair

MONKEY BUSINESS

I've just bashed out the complete works of E.L. James!

I THOUGHT YOU WERE HAVING A DRY JANUARY!

THIS IS DRY... IT'S A SAUVIGNON BLANC

Yes! It's the Gwyneth Paltrow Detox
by Our Nutrition Staff
Jan Diet

There's only one way to get rid of all the unwanted Gwyneth Paltrow in your life and that is to stop reading Goop online. Here's a simple guide on how to do it:

Day 1 Stop reading Goop online.

Day 2 Stop reading stuff about Goop online recycled in the Daily Mail.

Day 3 Stop reading Daily Mail stuff about Goop online recycled in all the other papers.

Day 4 Stop reading this.

And there you are... you're Gwyneth free! And you'll be happier, healthier, more energised and much less likely to feel sick.

The Adventures of Mr Milibean

Fountain & Jamieson

HOW DARE TONY BLAIR SAY I ALIENATE LARGE PARTS OF BUSINESS!

THERE ARE LARGE PARTS OF UK BUSINESS THAT THINK I'M COMPLETELY BRILLIANT!

SEE?

GOOD ON YOU, MILIBEAN!

KEEP UP THE GOOD WORK, MILIBEAN!

ANTI-DEPRESSANTS FACTORY

WELL DONE, ED!

CAN'T WAIT 'TIL YOU GET TO BE PRIME MINISTER!

HENRY DAVIES

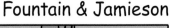

SUPERMODELS

KERBER

From The Message Boards

Members of the online community respond to the major issues of the day...

'Kiss-in' at Sainsbury's

Guys, I see that lesbians and gays held a mass protest at Sainsbury's in Brighton, after two women were asked to leave the shop for giving each other a "light kiss". Apparently a customer complained because she was "disgusted" and "worried for her child". The lesbians claim that the security guard (a lesbian herself) had "perpetrated a hate crime on behalf of Sainsbury's" by denying their "human right" to kiss. I must say I can't see how anyone could be offended by a peck on the cheek in in this day and age, but one newspaper pundit believes the couple have "opened a can of worms". If so, I hope they paid for them at the checkout! – *Bogbrush*

if you think it was just a peck on the cheek then get reel mate ☺ iv seen hundred's of lezzer film's an beleve me its not there face's they kiss 😊 – *hatfield gooner*

the supermarkit's want to drive a-way ordenry wite male's they stop u warin england shirt's they wont let u in with a can of beer in you'r hand 🌑 now u cant even wach 2 bird's snoggin wich is a thing evry normle bloke enjoy's 🌑 just cos some politicly corect homafobic nob complane's 🌑 if it was muslim's kissin or choppin head's of they woudnt bat an eyebrowe – *ENGLISH AND PROUD*

I see Sainsbury's has apologised to the couple. Perhaps they could issue them with a special "victim card", with double Nectar points. – *Brown out*

I saw a gay couple with a cucumber in their trolley, quite brazenly showing it off for the world to see. I felt sorry for the farmer who grew it, hoping it would be used in a nice salad or a sandwich. Imagine how he would feel if he knew it had ended up in a man's bottom. – *Christopher James*

People of the same sex kiss one another all the time in France, and it is considered perfectly normal. That's one reason why I never go there. – *I pay but have no say*

Two gay men were thrown off a London bus for kissing recently, and it shows that those of us with different lifestyles still face real discrimination. Only the other day on the tube several passengers were eating pungent fast food, yet people complained when I brought out a harmless salad containing human toes (consensually acquired, I might add, unlike their foul-smelling chicken and beef). – *Meat isn't necessarily murder*

Anyone noticed how the gay policemen and their surrogate "son" are keeping very quiet about all this? – *Metric Martyr*

Great stuff guys! And gays! – *Bogbrush*

AS SOME of us have long since recognised, the reason for the downing of AirAsia QZ8501 had nothing whatsoever to do with weather conditions in Surabaya, Indonesia, as the mainstream media have been trying to tell us.

As respected blogger *Truthfinder* points out, the third Malaysian plane to disappear within a year can hardly be a coincidence and there is plenty of evidence from radar scans that QZ8501 was well within the range of Russian top-secret MiG-94 stealth fighters operating out of Tajikistan air bases, which were almost certainly deployed by Putin to distract international attention from his latest covert operations along the eastern Ukraine-Russian border.

However, the authoritative *TwinTowerCIAcover-up* website has produced a mountain of evidence to show that the downing of the Air Asia A320 was the latest counter-move planned by Kim Jong-un's Silicon Valley-trained IT experts in revenge for Sony's provocative caricature of the Korean dictator, who, according to *ApolloIIfake*, has in fact been killed and replaced by a lookalike alien lizard who is now acting as a puppet of Beijing in a bid to destabilise the Russian rouble, which in turn will cause the collapse of the euro, leading to the destruction of the entire universe and *(cont. on other websites)*

Britain tackles Saudis over flogging

by Our Middle East Staff
Michael Buerka

The controversial issue of flogging in Saudi Arabia was raised by the British government in high level talks with the Saudi royal family.

Said a spokesman for the Foreign Office, "We told His Highness in the strongest possible terms that our position on flogging is clear. We're very keen on it. Whether it be missile systems, tanks, fighter jets, CS gas, water cannons, electric cattle prods, or whatever else they need, we'll flog it to them – no questions asked. Even the whips they need for flogging dissidents."

He continued, "We want this flogging to go on at least every two weeks for the rest of the

year, until lashings of money and whacking sums of cash have entered our accounts. With any luck, thanks to all this flogging, we will bleed them dry. We're flying the flog for Britain!"

A spokesman for human rights in Saudi Arabia said, "Aaaaaaaaaaaaaaaaaaargh!"

OIL PRICE DROP HITS RUSSIAN ECONOMY

Now everyone here has lost their shirt

POETRY CORNER

In Memoriam

Lee Kuan Yew,
Singapore's strong man.

Yes, you were
Famous for banning
Chewing gum.

Disappointingly for
Lovers of freedom
And irony, you
Did not come
To a sticky
End.

E.J. Thribb (17½)

Nursery Times

.... Friday, Once-upon-a-time ....

DAIRY CRISIS HITS NURSERYLAND

By Our Moos Staff

THE mounting disaster confronting the beleaguered milk industry has caused yet another farmer to abandon his dairy herd.

Old Macdonald, who had a farm, said that due to pressure on milk prices he was e-i-e-i-overdrawn and could no longer issue any more e-i-e-IOUs to the large supermarkets (particularly Lidl Boy Blue).

"I no longer have a farm," said Old Macdonald, "and on that farm I no longer have any

cows. There is no moo-moo here, no moo-moo there and, in fact, there is no moo-moo everywhere."

When asked what he had done with the cows, Old Macdonald confirmed that, due to the precarious and risky nature of the dairy industry, he was instead "going into space exploration".

"With my colleagues the cat (plus fiddle) and, of course, the little dog, I am going to send a cow over the moon."

....

Letter to the Editor of Nursery Times

Top Dignitaries Back Assisted Dying

Dear Sir,
We, the undersigned, are all very distinguished personages in our own fields and have accumulated years of expertise in the ethical implications of assisted dying.
It is our firm conclusion that this form of benign life termination help is both humanitarian and socially desirable and should be made legal throughout the realm of Nurseryland forthwith.

Yours sincerely,
The Wicked Stepmother, The Evil Queen, The Big Bad Wolf, Captain Hook, Farmer McGregor, The Giant up the Beanstalk, The Troll under the Bridge, The Witch in the Gingerbread House, The Queen of Hearts, Professor A.C. Grayling, And many others...

"They don't go into the risks when you have your eggs frozen"

WORLD LEADERS MARCH FOR FREE SPEECH

JE SUIS CHARLATAN!

EXCLUSIVE TO ALL NEWSPAPERS

Dear Cowardly Scumbags,

Why haven't you got the guts to print an offensive full-page cartoon of the Prophet Mohamed on your front page?

So much for your so-called commitment to free speech!

You are a disgrace to the memory of the Charlie Hebdo martyrs and your failure is a total and utter dereliction of duty and a craven and spineless surrender to the forces of evil. You make me sick.

Stand up and be shot, you hypocritical bastards.

(NAME & ADDRESS WITHHELD)

Louise Mensch 'Give Charlie a Knighthood'

Louise Mensch has taken to Twitter to urge the British Government to give slain cartoonist Charlie Hebdo an honorary knighthood.

"I consider Charlie Hebdo to be a personal friend, having met him a number of times at parties, and I demand we honour this great man and all he did to make us laugh by drawing Asterix for so many years," Mensch tweeted to her followers.

Once it was pointed out to her that Charlie Hebdo wasn't actually a person, Mensch insisted it had simply been a typo and she'd actually meant Rupert Murdoch.

Let's Parlez Franglais!

Numéro 94
Sur la fronte ligne

Monsieur Hollande: Bienvenue à la plus grande photo-opportunitée du monde.

Monsieur Cameron: Je suis Charlie.

Hollande: Vraiment? J'ai pensé que vous êtes David.

Madame Merkel: Ich bin Charlie.

Monsieur Hollande: C'est très confusant. Qui êtes-vous, monsieur homme noir avec l'amusant chapeau?

Le Président de Mali: Moi? Je suis Mali.

Hollande: Zut alors!

Prime Ministère de Turkey: Allowez-moi to explain. Nous sommes ici pour marcher contre le speech libre.

Hollande: Sûrement, vous meanez "pour" le speech libre.

L'Ambassadeur de Saudi Arabia: Non non, c'est contre. Il faut que nous crackons down sur les journalists et cartoonists.

Le Foreign Ministère Russe: Particulièrement si ils sont gaies.

L'Ambassadeur de Saudi Arabia: Ils ne peuvent pas dessiner sans hands!

Tous les despots: Hahahahahaha!

Cameron: Sacré bleu! Je suis dans le wrong place. Je should be next to la Première Ministre fruitée de Denmarke.

Madame Fruitée-Kinnock: Bonjour, grand garçon! Fancy un autre selfie inapproprié comme à la funèbre très longue de Monsieur Mandela?

Benjamin Netanyahu: Attendez un moment! Ne takez pas any photos sans moi!

Hollande: Vous n'êtes pas invited!

Netanyahu: Est-ce que c'est because je suis Jewish?

Hollande: C'est tout too confusant! Mon dieu!

L'Ambassadeur de Saudi: Vous blasphemez, infidel! Une mille de lashes pour vous.

Cameron: Vous ne pouvez pas say that!

Madame Fruitée-Kinnock: Oui, il peut! C'est le freedom de speech.

Hollande: Ma tête est spinning avec tous ces arguments philosophiques! Qu'est-ce qu'on peut say?

Photographier: Dîtes fromage!

Tout le monde: Je suis Cheesie!

© *Le late Kilometres Kington, 2015*

CAMERON ACTS ON FREEDOM OF SPEECH

by Our Political Staff **'Charlie' Moore**

PRIME Minister David Cameron last night pledged that his government would "stop at nothing" to protect the freedom of the press, which he described as "the very bedrock of our democracy".

"Not only," he told a small group of invited journalists, "am I prepared to go to France to have my photograph taken standing in the front row of three million people marching in support of free expression, I am also planning to introduce a whole range of new safeguards of our liberties, such as giving our security forces unprecedented new powers to monitor all citizens' mobile phones, emails, internet searches, Twitter accounts and any other form of social media interaction yet to be invented."

Taking liberties

"My government will at last enjoy the basic human right to know everything about everyone.

"This is the only way we can preserve our way of life against those who are set on eroding our long-cherished liberties, such as the right of journalists to have their emails intercepted in order to reveal their sources, particularly if they are writing rude things about the government, the police or any of those state agencies, whose only wish is to preserve the ancient *(cont. p94)*

THE CARTOONISTS' VIEW...

*"Do I still have the right **not** to offend, Miss?"*

AYiSS

"Make sure you get my funny side"

Royston
Je Suis Charlie

The cartoonists fight back with heavily labelled objects

"That's terrible, I normally just get a rejection slip"

ROGER LATHAM

KEY

I disapprove of what you say, but I will defend to the death your right to say it

Voltaire

Hot air

JE SUIS CHARLIE

cartoon dept.

"Twitter says, 'Draw Mohamed or I'll kill you'"

KenPyne

"We fired all our cartoonists years ago!"

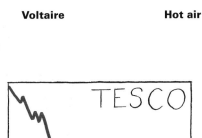

TESCO

George Leigh

Incendiary cartoon of the profit

BESTIE

THE EDITOR WAS TAKING NO CHANCES WITH ANYONE CALLED MUHAMMAD

Blair Claims 'On The Run' Letter Gives Immunity

by Our Northern Ireland Staff
Heinous O'Shamey

THE former prime minister Tony Blair yesterday stunned a Commons Committee when he suddenly took out of his pocket a letter, signed by himself, granting him lifetime immunity from prosecution for any crime he may have committed during his career.

Blair told the MPs, "It is very important that people who have been on the run for years should be allowed to live in peace, without the threat of arrest and trial hanging over them for the rest of their lives.

"For instance," he said, "I myself have been accused of the quite ridiculous crime of illegally invading Iraq, leading to the deaths of thousands of people.

"But my actions at that time were all part of the peace process that President Bush and I had launched in the Middle East –

and I think that's what we should remember.

"After all this time, to talk about putting people like myself on trial for war crimes would be to undo all the good that we did to bring peace and harmony to that troubled region."

Mr Blair assured the committee that he had put his life of criminal violence behind him:

"I promise you that I am now a completely law-abiding citizen, doing no harm to anyone.

"I now live a blameless life, flying round the world, making billions of pounds from corrupt dictators."

The committee thanked Mr Blair for giving them so much of his valuable time, to which he replied, looking at his watch, "That will be £375,000 an hour, payable to the *Tony Blair Straight Guy Foundation Trust* in Grand Cayman."

Chilcot report found on Mars

THERE was widespread joy throughout Westminster after hi-res images coming from the British Beagle 2 Mars Lander revealed it had crash-landed just metres from the Chilcot Inquiry report.

"We'd assumed that the Chilcot report had been lost forever, so you can imagine our delight at finding it intact and sitting on the surface of Mars," said everyone at Westminster.

"We know now the delay in its publication had nothing to do with politicians trying to cover their backs and everything to do with the fact that it has somehow found itself mysteriously marooned on the Red Planet."

Sources close to the Chilcot Inquiry say that with the first planned Nasa manned mission to Mars scheduled for 2030 it is

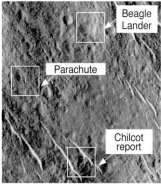

feasible that the report could be returned to Earth and published as early as 2035.

Politicians on all sides urged caution, however, saying a 2035 release date would mean that some of the politicians likely to face criticism would still be alive, so a publication date sometime around May 2055 was far more likely.

"Susan, the magician's back! I've no time to explain... just wait for me, ok?"

STEPHEN FRY WEDDING

I've got jokes older than you

Bless!

Film highlights

The Theory Of Winning Everything

Eddie Redmayne is confined to a wheelchair in order to solve one of the greatest mysteries of the universe – how do you win an Oscar?

As he wheels down the ramp with a Golden Globe, he thinks he's cracked the equation: 'Disability + Tears = Glory'. But little does he know that arch rival Benedict Cumberbatch is also working to crack the Osca Code, as a scientific genius with gay Asperger's. Suddenly, both are thrown off course by the appearance of Julianne Moore as an Alzheimer's victim who threatens to make the Academy forget all about the other contenders, particularly The Lego Movie, about which "everything is awesome" all of the time.

LED ZEP NEW GIRLFRIEND

We'll need a Stairlift To Heaven

(Continued Jimmy Page, 94)

POETRY CORNER

**In Memoriam
Dan Topolski**

So. Farewell
Then Dan Topolski,
Legendary rowing
Coach who took
Oxford to ten
Consecutive wins in
The boat race.

In, Out,
In, Out,
In, Out,
In,
Out.

Now we are all
Blue.

E.J. Thribb
(17½ strokes per minute)

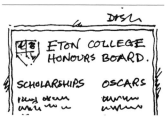

A Taxi Driver writes

EVERY week a well-known cab driver is invited to comment on an issue of topical importance. This week **Tom Watson** (Cab No. 49721) on the Historic Abuse Allegations circulating in Westminster.

Did you see that Leon Brittan finally snuffed it? Good riddance, I say. What a paedo. I mean, I haven't got any evidence that he was a paedo, but now he's dead I'm pretty sure that he must have been. Stands to reason. He must have been. Just Look at him: Tory. Big name in the Seventies. Friend of Mrs Thatcher. They're all paedos, aren't they? Makes you sick. No – I met this bloke in the pub and he swore blind that not only was he a paedo, but he also killed Diana. No – straight up! Here you are, guv, Gatwick. Oh sorry, did you say Heathrow? I had that Jimmy Savile in the back once. Very nice man.

Former Labour Grandee Pledges Support For Miliband

A statement by the Rt Hon Lord Prescott of Temple-Under-Desk

Let's face it, this Ed Miliband they've got running the Party is an unmitigable disaster. He goes poncing around like one of those Hampstead intellectualists when what the public want is plain-speaking common sense from someone who's lived in the real world up north.

No offence to Ed, but when it comes to a personalification contest, then he's got about as much charismability as a plate of mushy peas. No, if we're going to win this next election, which we are, then it won't be on Mibiland's popularitism, but on good, old-fashioned Labour party loyalty, which is why we've all got to stand four-squared beyond our leader, and do everything in our power not to undermine him as a useless, geeky little twerp.

© Lord Prescott 2015

New Chancellor of Winchester University – That Citation In Full

SALUTAMUS ALANUM TITCHMARSHUM FAMOSISSIMUM EXPERTUM HORTICULTICORICUM PER MULTOS ANNOS IN TELEVISIONE BBC COMMENTATOR EXPLICENDI ARTIS CULTIVATIONIS BEGONIAE, GLADIOLIQUE ET MULTIS FLORIBUS ATQUE VEGETALIBUS QUM RHUBARBI AUCTOREM INNUMERABILIS LIBROS SPINOFFORUM ET IN "ARTIBUS PERSICIS" VIZ ARSLIKHANIIS EXPERTISSIMUS CUM DUCO EDINBURGHO PRINCEPS CAROLUS ETCETERA GROVELLARIUS OBSEQUIO NAUSEATICUM GAUDEAMUS!

© Universitatum Venta Belgarum (formerly St Alfred's Catering College) 2015.

The Gnome POPE PUNCH BAG

No more "turning the other cheek" misery with the new must-have Vatican-approved boxing accessory – perfect for the papist pugilist!

Someone insult your mother? **Pow!**

Someone challenge your religious beliefs? **Biff!**

Someone suggest that actually the peacemakers are the ones who are going to be blessed? **Wham!**

Yes! Show off your muscular Christianity with the **Pope Punch Bag™**

> As the Good Book says, "The wise man built his house upon the Rocky III"

£199.99
(from all good Christian bookshops)

Millions of people sigh and say, 'Just as I was starting to really like this Pope' by Bear Shitzinwoods

PEOPLE all over the world have received a cruel reminder that the Pope is, after all, a Catholic. After many commentators had noticed the new Pope saying sensible things about gays, women, abortions, divorces and climate change, people had started to question whether Pope Francis was a Catholic at all, many of them saying to each other things like, "If all the popes were like this one, I'd actually vote for them."

Now, tragically, the world has been reminded that the Pope is just one of a large number of people who say you can't make fun of the extremely serious business of religion without provoking a violent (cont. p94)

"Men!"

The Daily Terrorgraph

JIHADI JOHNSON WRITES

Cripes! That's the trouble with these extremist chaps – all they think about is sex! Sex, sex, sex! I mean, take that Boris Johnson fellow – he's clearly gagging for it the whole time, which makes him jolly angry and frustrated, so he tries to take over the world!!

No wonder he comes over as a loony and talks nonsense... he's too busy thinking about getting his legover with 72 non-virgins! Blimey!

If only he could stop trying to have sex all day and try a bit of celibacy then we'd all sleep happier in our beds rather than someone else's! Crikey.

© The Daily Terrorgraph 1436

"Isn't it great, we're being bombed back into the Dark Ages?"

Fundamentalist attacks religious building

by Our Religious Staff
Libby Womens

Today an extremist radical fanatic from the Church of England stormed into York Minister, hurling a mild objection at the Archbishop of York, Dr John Sentamu, during the ordination of the first woman Bishop.

As terrified onlookers turned around with a look of mild surprise and tutted, the "lone wolf" unleashed a barrage of well-mannered criticism, claiming there was no biblical authority for women bishops.

When asked to leave, the dangerous militant, from the fringe of the C of E, immediately left quietly by a side door. And the service continued almost as if nothing had happened.

This is only the latest outrage in the long-running civil war which is tearing Anglicanism apart, and threatening the stability of the whole of the Middle England, disrupting coffee mornings and *(cont. Psalm 94)*

BIBLICAL TIMES

Apple to blame for downfall of mankind

BY JENNY SIS

The hugely successful knowledge delivery system, the Apple, was last night blamed for everything that is wrong with the human race.

The Apple has proved incredibly successful, shifting up to one unit in its first seven days. An early adopter of the Apple, Eve, said ,"It's a classic – the design is so sleek and shiny, and the marketing was far too tempting." She added, "Actually I didn't really need it, life was perfect without it. But now I've got the taste for it, I want every size of Apple available."

Eve's husband Adam was unavailable for comment because he was too busy toiling and delving to pay for the Apple upgrade.

SINFORMATION TECHNOLOGY

A spokesman for Apple, Mr Serpent, said, "Okay, so the Apple comes with a very high price of eternal exile from Eden, separation from God and the burden of original sin, but apart from that it's pretty much a bargain." He continued, "We're just satisfying demand – except any demand for tax, obviously – which should be forwarded to our new offshore base: c/o our accountant B.L. Zebub and Partners, The Lake of Fire, Seventh Circle of Hell (Luxembourg)."

"We'll see how unlimited this broadband really is..."

FEBRUARY 6TH 2015

THE TIMES OF LONDON

London's Cranes Dip in Tribute to Greatest Leader the World Has Ever Seen

by Our Funeral Staff **Robert Grave** and **Crem Attlee**

BRITAIN came to a respectful standstill yesterday to mark the passing of one of the great statesmen of the modern era.

Flags flew at half-mast, muffled church bells tolled from Westminster Abbey, and mourners in black queued to sign books of condolence.

All were trying to come to terms with the death of a man they'd never heard of, the late King Abdullah of Saudi Arabia, the world's richest oil-producing state.

Within hours, world leaders were flying into Riyadh to express their deep grief at the death of the man whom their aides had told them to describe as "the Revered Father of his People, the Guardian of the Holy Places and the Keeper of the World's Money".

Leading the mass turnout of global dignitaries was President Barack Obama, who said, "At a time of national tragedy like this, it would be quite out of place to talk about trivial matters, such as human rights and this poor guy who they've been whipping to death for blogging against the Saudi regime."

He was accompanied by Secretary of State John Kerry, who stepped off the plane carrying a placard reading "Je Suis Charlie" and saying that he just wished to give "all you people in France-land a big hug".

He was promptly arrested by security police and stoned to death, along with Michelle Obama for her failure to comply with the Saudi funeral "burqas only" dress code.

Also present was the British prime minister Dave Cameron, who said, "This very sad time is a perfect opportunity for me to say how sorry we are at the loss of the finest customer our arms industry has ever known."

Prince Charles, representing his mother, said, "The late King, like me, was a great believer in inter-faith harmony, as we can see throughout the Middle East today."

Mr Tony Blair, representing one of his foundations, the Kazakhstan Growth Fund, stressed the late King's remarkable contribution to Middle Eastern peace.

"His late Majesty," he said, "was nearly as influential in maintaining the stability of the region as myself."

Ms Christiane Lagarde, representing the International Monetary Fund, paid particular tribute not just to the King's large pile of money, but also the wonderful reforms he brought in to further the cause of women's rights.

"His late Majesty," she explained, "was personally responsible for reducing the punishment for driving a car before sunset during Ramadan from instant beheading to the much more civilised 1,000 lashes, before having your head cut off."

After the late King's remains had been buried in an unmarked grave, the world leaders were given audience by the late King's successor, his half-brother, Salman ben Rushdie.

The new king has vowed to continue with his brother's modernising agenda and to drag Saudi Arabia kicking and screaming into the 14th century.

What the Greek elections tell us about our election

by Our Man in Athens
Harry Stophaneeze

THE election of Alexis Tsipras's far left Syriza party in Greece is clearly a warning to politicians of all persuasions that the public is tiring of austerity, undoubtedly benefitting those parties on the left, unless of course Syriza's election actually lays bares the folly of abandoning austerity, meaning it would instead benefit those parties on the right, unless of course Syriza and the Troika come to a compromise, which would suggest there is a middle way, benefiting those parties here on the centre, unless of course the real beneficiaries are the anti-politics parties...unless this results in a backlash against them, or...err umm, oh God, is that 5,000 words yet...unmm... something about Greece being the birthplace of democracy...umm... maybe an Aristotle quote...err.... something about cheap holidays... ummm...Isn't it sad about Demis Roussos?...Perhaps the real lesson for British politicians is that Greek politics have nothing to do with our election and...*(cont for 5,000 words)*

"Woke up this morning – which is unusual for me these days because I have been sleeping badly due to a lot of stress and stuff, so I don't get off until about four or five and then of course it's often midday or even later before I wake up"

Nursery Times

Friday, Once-upon-a-time

OWL AND PUSSYCAT IN HAVEN SCAM

by Our Financial Staff **Robin Cock**

THERE was outrage in Nurseryland today when it was revealed that the Owl and the Pussycat had gone offshore in order to avoid paying their taxes.

They sneaked out of the country in a beautiful pea green boat, in order to invest their honey and "plenty of money" which was cunningly wrapped up in a five-pound note.

On arrival at their chosen tax haven, the land where the Bong tree grows, they planned to further outfox the Nurseryland fiscal authorities by getting married purely for the tax benefits accrued.

They took advice from a local piggy-wiggy banky-wanky, which provided a ring for the ceremony. For this the Owl and the Pussycat paid a mere shilling, via a holding company in NeverNeverLand, thus releasing shareholdings in the Rumpelstiltskin gold-spinning trust, resulting in a negative transfer of funds at a preferential rate of interest, which meant that they made an overall loss for the tax year in question.

"Myself and the Owl, who's an elegant fowl, have done nothing illegal," purred the Pussycat, while the Owl hooted with laughter all the way to the bank of Bongtree.

Continued the Pussycat, "The arrangements were all supervised by the authorities in question, namely the Turkey who lives on the hill". But critics have been quick to point the finger, saying, "It's just another tax-avoiding Fat Cat (and Owl) attempting to justify their greed, while they stuff their faces on mince, and slices of quince, all eaten with a runcible spoon, which is no doubt silver and subsidised by the hardworking honest folk of Nurseryland."

The Owl and the Pussycat were unavailable for further comment, as they were too busy dancing by the light of the moon, the moon, at the Fairy Tory Black and White Ball.

Physics Graduation

BANKS LATEST

We're too big to jail!

TORY PARTY ROCKED BY NEW FINANCIAL SCANDAL

by Our Money Staff **Eve Asion** and **Phil Boots**

THERE was shock this week as it was revealed that one Tory businessman had been secretly funnelling money into HMRC.

The complex procedure involved filling in a quite simple form, finding an honest accountant, and then submitting the form before the 31st of January. The money was then siphoned off quite unmysteriously from the businessman's own bank account into the coffers of HMRC.

Said one expert, "This is quite clearly a deliberate attempt to avoid avoiding tax." The episode sent shock waves through Westminster, as the businessman was named and shamed by a parliamentary select committee.

Said the chancellor, George Osborne, "This is blatant tax paying and will not be tolerated from anyone connected to the Tory Party."

The Prime Minister added, "I promise to clamp down on this sort of thing. Unfortunately, there are always a few good apples in the barrel who ruin it for everyone else." The businessman has gone into hiding – sorry, gone into work as normal.

THE HSBC SCANDAL
THE EYE'S MOST READ STORIES

Nazi investors shocked

Retired Nazis have spoken of their shock at discovering that their private Swiss banks have been involved in tax avoidance.

"My late father invested his large cache of gold in Switzerland in good faith, never thinking for a minute that the Swiss could be up to no good and defrauding the British taxpayer," said Adolf Hitler, speaking from his home in Argentina.

"If you can't trust highly secretive Swiss banks to be scrupulously above board and trustworthy, then who can you trust?"

Avoidance 'shocks public'

There was growing anger today amongst the public as the full extent of HBSC avoidance became clear.

"It seems that all HSBC bankers caught up in this Swiss scandal, from Chief Executive Stephen Green down, have completely avoided jail," said one horrified member of the public.

"Avoidance of jail on an industrial scale such as this is staggering."

Lessons must be learned about lessons not being learned

The Banking Ombudsman said today that Britain's banks must learn lessons from the HSBC banking scandal which it didn't learn from the Barclays scandal or the Lloyds scandal before that or the RBS scandal before that or the one before that or the one before that or the Northern Rock scandal before that.

"It's vital we learn the lessons we didn't learn all those other times this time, so that when the next scandal comes along we can say that lessons have been learned from not learning the lessons they were supposed to have learned last time."

HEIR OF SORROWS

by Dame Sylvie Krin, author of *Duchess of Hearts* & *You're Never Too Old*

THE STORY SO FAR: Prince Charles has had a number of unfortunate misunderstandings whilst in the bath, leading him to imagine that his hour of destiny has arrived and leading to severe subsequent disappointment. Now read on…

THE hot bubbles foamed and frothed around the weary royal shoulders, as Prince Charles slumped in his new authentic Wolf Hall-style outdoor Jacuzzi, an exact replica of the original Tudor Hotte Tubbe which he was developing for his new Duchy Original Organic Bathtime Experience Brand. But the soothing water jets did little to relax the furrowed royal brow as Charles read through a soggy advance copy of a controversial new book about him entitled *The King of Hearts* by Catty Mayerkitup.

"This book is… I don't know how to describe it… 'appalling' doesn't seem to be strong enough".

"How about 'really appalling', sire?" suggested Sir Alan Fitztightly, his Aide-de-Very-Camp who was was dutifully turning the pages.

"I mean this suggestion that I don't like criticism and have fits of despair… I just don't like it. It makes me…"

"Despair, my liege?" added Sir Alan, unhelpfully. Charles ignored him and turned his attentions instead to his latest bath novelty, a large model aircraft carrier which was an exact replica of the as yet unbuilt Royal Navy flagship named after him, HMS Prince Charles.

"Are you sure it came with no aeroplanes?" a worried Charles asked, testily.

"Absolutely, sire, the manufacturers were quite adamant."

Charles eased back in the tub and his breath formed small clouds of steam in the cold January air.

"I'm not sure that this whole hot-and-cold bath experience thingy works," he grumbled.

"Indeed not, Boss," agreed Sir Alan, who doubled as the Keeper of the Back Scratcher Royale, shivering slightly in his ornamental britches and shoes, as he stood beside the hot tub in the middle of the Multi-Faith Maze at Highgrove, watching over the lightly poaching figure of the heir to the throne. "And I don't think we want to read any more of this nonsense, do we?" said the silver-tongued diplomat, deftly removing the book

and throwing it into the Thomas Cranmer Tudor Martyr log-burning stove, which ecologically powered Ye Hotte Tubbe.

"Quite so. Isn't it time for repeats of *The Goon Show* on Radio 4 Extra Plus One?" enquired the monarch-to-be. "I think it's the one where Colonel Bloodnock eats a curried egg and explodes."

"Indeed it is, sire," replied Sir Alan, adjusting the new iPad Heir which he had brought along, anticipating exactly this request. "I'll just touch this little fellow and see what happens… as Backstairs Billy used to say to the new underfootmen in the dear old days of…"

"Yes, thank you very much, Sir Alan," Charles interrupted his valet's off-colour banter testily. "And make sure you don't get any of that ghastly rolled-up news… one needs time to escape the modern world."

But as Sir Alan busied himself with the new technology, Charles found himself listening not to the humorous singing of *Kim Yong Rod Liddle I Po*, but the unwelcome sound of the newsreader Charlotte Greenpeace, as her sober tones filled the frosty air.

"And here's the main news again… the world's oldest monarch has finally died… a figure who for so long represented continuity of tradition and religious authority, yet who did so much to modernise the Royal Family…"

"Hang on, hang on!" shouted Sir Alan, as an exultant Prince Charles leapt out of the bath, grabbing a towel bearing the legend Crown Jewels Under Here (a souvenir his son Harry had brought back from Las Vegas) and placing it around his waist. The gallant aircraft carrier sank beneath the displaced waves of bath water, but Charles did not look back.

"This is it! One's time has finally come! Vivat Rex Activistus!"

"Just wait a minute, sire," pleaded Sir Alan. "It may not be what you think."

The news continued solemnly, "The throne passes to a younger brother…"

"What? To Andrew? I don't believe it!" Charles shouted at the darkening skies. "I'm going to write someone a really stiff letter." And with that he was gone, already running back towards the main house. Sir Alan was left alone and gently switched off the rest of the broadcast about the sad death of King Abdullah of Saudi Arabia.

As he watched the semi-naked figure of the Prince sprinting past the ornamental ha-ha, the Royal Equerry-As-Folk smiled and thought, "Ha-ha!"… "Ha-ha-ha-ha-ha…"

(To be continued)

HONEYSETT R.I.P.

"You can do the entire degree course online these days, including the graduation ceremony"

"And I'm not at all happy about them playing 'Jenga' in their lunch break"

"I appreciate that his full-body tattoos were expensive, but I'm afraid we don't have the facilities to skin him"

DIARY

JEFFREY ARCHER

This past week, in India, I visited six cities in seven days. I was surprised and delighted to find out how popular I am in the world-famous sub-continent, which was ruled over by Britain for over a thousand years.

It's an extraordinary feeling, to be greeted at Bangalore airport by up to 50,000 people waving copies of one's latest novel, "A Pack of Lies". The book has, incidentally, already sold just under 350,000,000 worldwide. Excellent news – or so my accountants inform me!

Visiting seven cities in six days certainly takes it out of you – or would do, if I weren't in such excellent shape. My excellent personal trainer, Jacqui, insists I have the body of a man half my age.

That's not to say I haven't slowed down a bit. When I was a student at Oxford University, I used to run a mile twice a day in just over three minutes, though I've always kept this true statistic under my hat, to spare the blushes of my slowcoach friend, poor old Roger Bannister!

India can be an exhausting place, particularly if, like me, you've just visited eight cities in five days.

My next novel is set in India. It's a powerful tale of two twins, Chang and Sanjay, separated by fate but reunited by destiny.

In time, one ends up the Prime Minister of China and the other ends up King of India. Not bad, for two little boys who started life begging in rags on the backstreets of the city of Alabama!

The action swings between the Taj Mahal, where one brother lives, and the Great Wall of China, where the other has a flat. I'm famous for my research, so I spent ten hours a day, seven days a week, fifty two weeks a year for three years being guided around those two excellent countries by leading experts in their fields.

Young novelists do please take note: research pays dividends. Without it, I would never have discovered that the languages they speak in India and China are entirely different. Did you know that, without a highly-skilled interpreter, an Indian won't have the foggiest what a Chinaman is saying to him, and vice versa?

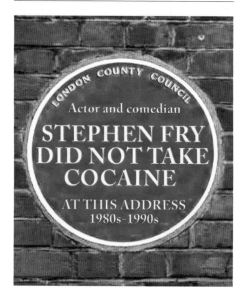

In an extraordinary twist of fate both twins are appointed to their jobs – head of India, head of China – on exactly the same day. Only when their photos are printed next to each other in world-famous newspaper *The Washington Times* do they realise they must be long-lost brothers.

I wrote 27 drafts of their reunion before I got it exactly right. It's those expert touches of local colour – language, food, and so on – that are vitally important if you want to become a worldwide bestseller, translated into over 2,546 languages, at the last count.

The twins finally meet up in an excellent international restaurant. Literary scholars tell me that my accuracy of the telling detail is quite masterly. Note, for instance, how Chang eats with chopsticks. The reason? Right first time: he is Chinese.

"Velly nicey to meety you" exclaimed Chang, the eldest twin by a matter of minutes. He was speaking perfect Chinese as he brought out his excellent chopsticks to eat his gourmet Chop Suey.

"Velly nicey to meety you, too" exclaimed Sanjay, tucking into his excellent Chicken Tikka Masala, an exotic curry dish from his homeland. He had been speaking the Indian language fluently since he was born, nine months after he was conceived by his mother and father in that night of passion.

The two brothers embraced, tears flooding out of their eyes. Looking at his brother's tears, Sanjay was reminded of the River Ganges in his beloved homeland, India, and at that very same time Chang was reminded of the Yangtse, which flows excellently through China. And as their tears poured out onto their meals, they both realised one thing: this was a reunion that was truly emotional.

Having visited nine cities in India in the past four days, believe me I am pretty exhausted! But the sheer unadulterated enthusiasm of my 750,437,920 devoted readers in India for scenes such as the above definitely spurs me on!

Between delivering the keynote address to the Indian parliament (standing room only) and signing 20,000 copies of my book in the course of a single morning, I devoted my time to polishing up my sentences.

Take the above example – "The two brothers embraced, tears flooding out of their eyes". I kid you not when I tell you that this particular sentence went through 15 drafts before I got it right. I wasn't happy with "flooded" and knew there must be something better. So I sat and polished. First, the tears ran out of their eyes, then they dropped out of their eyes, then they cascaded, sprang, poured, shot, roared, gushed, bounced, dribbled, hopped, danced and galloped. It was only when I switched on the TV news and saw a Nasa test flight that that the perfect word finally came to me: rocketed.

A word of advice. No story-teller ever got anywhere without giving his sentences a good polish. It's what I've been telling fans in ten cities in India over the past three days – it's not just about picking the right words, you've also got to put them in the right order. The right words in the wrong order may gain you critical plaudits and the so-called Booker Prize – but, believe you me, my friend, the general public are not so easily fooled!

As told to
CRAIG BROWN

JON & MICK / MODERN TOSS

didn't I give this to you for Christmas?

yeah I didn't like it, happy birthday

1 FOR THE PRICE OF 2

we thought it was worth a try, a lot of our customers are heavy drinkers

we're a bit short staffed at the moment do you mind interviewing yourself for the vacancy?

INVESTMENT ADVICE

There is this option, but I have to warn you it's very high risk

isn't that a fruit machine?

have one of our loyalty cards, I've already stamped it for this one

1938...

Daily Mail

SEPTEMBER 30, 1938

APPEASEMENT SOUND POLICY — HITLER IS 'JOLLY GOOD CHAP'

by Our Proprietor the **Viscount Rothermere**

ANYONE who suggests that Herr Hitler is a mad dictator who is posing a threat to the peace of Europe is just an irresponsible and dangerous warmonger.

Herr Hitler was perfectly within his rights to annex Austria and absorb it into the greater Germany, on the grounds that the population was almost entirely German speaking and loved German food, particularly wurst and Wienerschnitzel.

The German leader is hugely popular at home, particularly after his brilliantly successful hosting of the Olympic Games.

But it is particularly absurd to suggest that Herr Hitler is a crazed megalomaniac whose only ambition is to take over the rest of Europe. He is merely a patriotic and conservative statesman, driven by a desire to further the interests of his people and the country he loves.

2015...

Daily Mail

FRIDAY, February 20, 2015

TIME TO STOP APPEASEMENT — PUTIN WORSE THAN HITLER

by Our Editor **Paul Dacre** (with the full support of his proprietor the Viscount Rothermere)

ANYONE who can't see that Vladimir Putin is a mad dictator who is posing a threat to the peace of Europe is just an irresponsible and dangerous appeaser.

Mr Putin outraged the world with his ruthless decision to annex Crimea and absorb it into his greater Russia, on the ridiculous grounds that the population was almost entirely Russian speaking and loved Russian food, particularly borscht

and vodka *(subs, please check)*.

The Russian leader may be hugely popular at home, particularly after his supposedly successful hosting of the Olympic Games, but it is particularly absurd to deny that Mr Putin is a crazed megalomaniac whose only ambition is to take over the rest of Europe.

Mr Putin may wish to pose as a patriotic and conservative statesman, driven by a desire to further the interests of his people and the country he loves. But to believe this would be as ridiculous as to believe the rubbish we were writing back in 1938.

UKRAINE LATEST

Ready... Aim... Ceasefire!

The Eye's Controversial New Columnist

The columnist who exposed the scandal the newspapers dubbed "Cowandgate"

This week I am *très en colère* about a French court preventing a couple from naming their baby "Nutella", claiming that it was "against the child's interests". Zut alors! This is political correctness gone *dementie*l! Firstly, the freedom-hating socialists try to name every single person in the country "Charlie" and now this! Speaking as a baby *(see photo)*, I can categorically state that there is NO form of Christian name that serves as an impediment to ANY child's prospects – provided it is coupled with the right-sounding surname. Possibly a child called "Nutella Bloggs" or "Nutella Jones" would have some problems. But if, say, it is called "Nutella Lawson" then *(cont. p94)*

BRUCIE SLAMS DEATH DUTIES

by Our Showbiz Staff
Jenny Raytiongame

SIR Bruce Forsyth today broke BBC impartiality guidelines by launching a devastating tirade against so-called death taxes.

"It isn't nice to see them," quipped Sir Brucie. "To see them it isn't nice." But beneath his trademark humour, the national treasure was deadly serious.

"If I am to be taxed every time I go on stage and die, then I will have no money left."

He continued, "I will have to leave the country and take my elderly jokes to somewhere where they understand the need to pass on an accumulated inheritance of comedy gold."

POETRY CORNER

In Memoriam Michele Ferrero, confectionery tycoon

So. Farewell
Then Michele Ferrero,
The man who gave
Us Ferrero Rocher at the
Ambassador's Reception.

"Monsieur... you are
Really spoiling us."
That was your
Catchphrase,
Though perhaps "You
Are spoiling our
Teeth" would have been
More accurate.

You also gave us
Kinder Eggs, which
To our teeth
Were no
Kinder.

E.J. Thribb (17½ fillings)

NO PROPHET WAS KEPT IN THIS WHALE OVERNIGHT

McLACHLAN

PUTIN TO INVESTIGATE MURDER OF OPPOSITION LEADER

I shall do everything in my power to find the killer

EU-phemisms

"We will support Ukraine as we'd support an EU nation state"

We'll provoke a crisis then drop you in it

MPs slam BBC

by Our Media Correspondent
Hugh Cantalk

A panel of MPs today launched a scathing attack on the BBC, during which they tore into what they called "a failing institution that was no longer fit for purpose".

One MP told BBC chiefs, "You lot are a total waste of public money. You're engulfed by one scandal after another, and are increasingly detached from the real world.

"Nobody trusts you, as you pursue your own agenda, feathering your own nests with inflated salaries. It's hard to think of any other national body or group of people who the public hate more.

"Oh. Hang on. Er... I've just thought of one. You're not recording this are you?"

'YES, IT'S WAR...' SAYS CAMERON, '...TIME FOR OUR BOYS TO GO IN'

by Our Defence Staff **Evelyn Waughmonger**

DAVID CAMERON last night issued the sternest challenge yet to Russia's President Putin, whom he described as a ruthless aggressor who clearly cannot wait to take over the world.

"Someone has to stand up to this crazed lunatic before it is too late," said Mr Cameron, "which is why it has once again fallen to Britain to defend the free world.

"I am therefore going to send a really strong message to the Russian dictator, by deploying no fewer than twelve British frontline troops to the western Ukraine, equipped with a state-of-the-art personnel carrier, but only on the condition that they take no part in any unpleasant military action and keep well away from any advancing Russians."

Defence experts have nevertheless criticised Mr Cameron's robust move, by pointing out that twelve men now constitute almost the entire British army, and that they will be hugely overstretched if in June they have to be recalled to take part in Trooping the Colour.

'Why the Tories are Committed to Universal Pensioner Benefits' in Full

Old people vote

'Never been a better time to get a mortgage'

by Our Housing Correspondent
Pat Chance

NEW figures have revealed that there's never been a better time for first-time buyers to get a mortgage to top up the deposit they can't afford.

"This will come as a huge relief to all the people who can't afford a house because we forgot to build any for the last twenty years," said an estate agent, rubbing his pinstriped suit gleefully.

"It's tremendous news. And, although nobody can afford to get a mortgage, presuming you have the hundreds of thousands of pounds required for a no-bed flat thirty miles from the nearest toilet, you'll be able to secure an extremely competitive rate for it."

The Adventures of Mr Milibean

Fountain & Jamieson

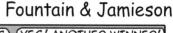

The Jihadi John I Knew

BY EVERYONE

HE was the kindest, gentlest shyest extremist ever to behead someone in cold blood.

When I knew him all those months ago, he was a delightful, polite young man who wouldn't have hurt a fly. Unfortunately, flies weren't the problem, as we found out later.

However, in those days he was a model student and I distinctly remember him helping old ladies to cross the road.

Sadly, on many occasions, he helped them into the face of oncoming traffic, but he always did his best to warn the aged pedestrians by shouting a friendly warning, such as "Die, infidel!".

He was a lovely lad and when he worked in IT he was always happy to help other youngsters with their computer problems. I remember one particular time when someone came in, wanting to know how to access an obscure Islamicist website containing bomb-making instructions and Jihadi John, as we knew him then, couldn't have been more considerate, as he lent the customer his balaclava and shouted "Allahu Akbar!", surprising another waiting customer who was hoping to get an upgrade on his graphics package.

But then, that was the kind of lovely, warm, charming psychopath (cont. p94)

"I say... weren't we radicalised at school together?"

ROBERT THOMPSON

Was Ernst Blofeld Radicalised by MI6?

by Our Supervillain Correspondent
Quentin Threats

CLOSE friends of Ernst Stavro Blofeld have insisted that Ernst was a quiet, friendly, studious chap and that his desire to bring Western civilisation to its knees only happened as a result of numerous encounters with James Bond.

"There can be no doubt that the continual harassment he suffered at the hands of James Bond is what turned Blofeld into the villain we now know him to be," insisted close friend Rosa Klebb.

"Ernst was just going about his business, peacefully planning world domination from his secret undersea lair, but James Bond just wouldn't leave him alone.

"It got to the point where Ernst was completely paranoid, he felt he was being suffocated, he

didn't know which of his orange-suited henchmen would suddenly introduce themselves to him out of the blue as Bond, James Bond.

"But for MI6 and James Bond harassing him, I'm certain Blofeld and his global criminal organisation SPECTRE would never have caused anyone the slightest bit of trouble."

SYRIA BUS STOP DRAMA

2015-02-18 02:25:04

You wait ages for a Jihadi schoolgirl bride and then 3 come along at once

---

ISIS teenagers: Why can't we just let them be?

by **Yasmin Provides-anyone-with-an-Alibi Brown**

WHY oh why is everyone criticising these young girls for going off to the Middle East?

They've just done exactly what teenagers have always done – fallen in love with romantic, dangerous idols.

This is a tale as old as teenagerdom itself. Just think of the 1950s, when girls fell madly in love with such menacing, warlike figures as Bill Haley and the Comets or the thrillingly dangerous Pat Boone. What's so wrong with that?

Before we start wagging our fingers at these girls, we must remember that young women have always found themselves excited by murderers, such as the Beatles when they appeared on the Ed Sullivan show.

Those idols were just as transgressive as ISIS in their way. It's basically no different these days to want to travel thousands of miles across the world to wage a holy war, establish a Caliphate and murder anyone who disagrees with you.

Who is this terrifying English speaking Muslim radical known only as 'George'?

HERNERADI

INTRODUCING THE EYE'S NEW COLUMNIST

GLEN SLAGG

Fleet Street's Man Friday??!!

■ POLDARK??!! Phwoar!?! I would!! Wouldn't you?!? I'm talkin' about Aidan Turner playing Captain Ross on the BBC's sizzling Sunday night sexorama!? I'm normally as straight as the next bloke, but one sight of this tousle-haired, tricorn-hatted tough guy with his shirt off makes me want to join the Cornish Village People !?! Geddit!?! I'd like to!!?! Geddit!?!!

■ POLDARK!?! Talk about a Turner

on!?! Geddit!? I'm as heterosexual as the next man (Robert Crampton, David Aaronovitch, etc) but ravishing raunchy Ross has reawakened my inner Gok Wan!?! Those shirts!?! Those breeches?!? That mascara scar!! Mmmm!!? I'd like to be a Cornish pasty so Randy Ross could gobble me up!?! Poldark??! I'd like to hold his pole in the dark *(This is rubbish. You're fired, Ed. I'm bringing back Glenda)*.

GLENDA SLAGG

Fleet Street's Girl Friday??!!

■ POLDARK??!! Phwoar!?! I would!! Wouldn't you?!? Ravishing Raunchy Ross has left us gals a-droolin' and a-dribblin' on a Sunday night!!?! Mmm... I'm not Turnering him off!!? Geddit!?!! I wish he'd come to my Aidan tell

me that he's all mine (not of the tin variety!! Geddit??!!) I wish I was a Cornish ice cream, then I would melt as he licked me all over *(This is rubbish. You're fired as well, Ed.)*

Byeee!!

Social Care Scandal
Elderly lady has fall

by Our Pensioner Staff **Brit Ekland**

An elderly lady last night suffered a nasty fall while trying to climb up a short flight of stairs in a public building. Observers were appalled that there was no railing to help her, and that she had been given unsuitable shoes for a lady of her advancing years.

The lady, known globally as Old Ma Donna, was happily singing to herself, when a cloak she was

wearing to keep out the cold got snagged, and caused her to take a nasty tumble. None of the carers rushed to help her, as they were all dancing around on all fours, wearing devil masks, rendering them incapable of offering any assistance.

These shocking scenes were fortunately caught on camera, or else this sort of neglect might easily have passed unnoticed. The CQC admitted that the O2 Stadium should have been given a thorough Health and Safety check, as it was well known to be frequented by elderly people, such as Status Quo, the Eagles and Paul McCartney.

 # *Dave Snooty* AND HIS NO PALS

Dispatches

That Transcript in Full

(Blurred shot of the Rt Hon Sir Malcolm Rifkind MP sitting at a desk in office)

Blonde female reporter: Sir Malcolm, you are obviously a very important and powerful politician...

Rifkind: Yes, I certainly am.

Blonde: Would you like a very large sum of money for not having to do very much work?

Rifkind: Yes, I would.

Blonde: Could you say that again for me, and speak into this briefcase on the desk?

Rifkind: How much money are we talking about? My usual rate is £5,000 a minute – does that sound reasonable?

Blonde: Yes, it sounds great, but could you speak up a bit?

Rifkind: I'd be really happy to get all this money from you because, as an MP, I'm very badly paid, and really I just work for myself. But this means that I've got loads of free time, so you can definitely count me in. Who are your clients again?

Blonde: Oh, they're a new firm called SCAM, which stands for South China Asset Management. You can check

them out on our website, which we put up yesterday.

Rifkind: I've no need to do that because, before you came, I rang a chap I know who used to work in Hong Kong, and he said that although he'd never heard of your company, it sounded pretty kosher.

Blonde: Ha ha ha ha. Well, thank you, Sir Malcolm. I think we've got everything we need.

(Cut to the offices of the Rt Hon Jack Straw)

Blonde: Mr Straw, you're obviously a very important and powerful politician, not to mention very handsome.

Straw: Yes, I certainly am.

Blonde: Would you like us to pay you a very large sum of money for doing very little?

Straw: That seems very reasonable. I'm not, of course, one of those ghastly MPs who call themselves "cabs for hire", like my poor ex-friend Stephen Byers, who stupidly got caught when some unscrupulous reporter put a briefcase on his desk and asked him to talk into it. That was incredibly stupid of him. I would never fall for a cheap trick like that.

Blonde: Of course not, Mr Straw. You're far too clever.

Straw: So, how much money are you talking about? My usual rate is £5,000 for the first mile, and then we negotiate a fee for the rest, with a discount for Gatwick.

Blonde: Thank you, Mr Straw. I think we've got all we need.

This programme is a repeat, and will be repeated again ad nauseam...

The Daily Telegraph

FRIDAY, MARCH 6, 2015

Comment

THE DAILY TELEGRAPH

Established 1855

The nation has rightly been deeply shocked by the revelations that the representatives of one of the country's most trusted and respected institutions have allowed grubby commercial temptations to overrule their professional integrity.

Ruthless greed is always an unattractive human trait. But when it is accompanied by secrecy, hypocrisy and a wholesale abandonment of moral principle, it threatens seriously to undermine the very foundations of our democracy.

We are not of course talking here about Sir Malcolm Rifkind and Mr Jack Straw. No, we are talking about ourselves, caught red-handed by a fearless Telegraph journalist Mr Peter Oborne in the act of allowing our lust for advertising revenue to dictate our coverage of some of the biggest and most controversial stories of our time, particularly HSBC.

That is why we demand that there should be no inquiry into this scandalous betrayal of public trust and there should be no resignations from the board or senior management of the Telegraph Media Group. Furthermore, we will do everything in our power to ensure that this editorial is never published.

Letters to the Editor

SIR – I notice with a heavy heart that standards in the Telegraph have, indeed, fallen precipitously in the last few months.

I refer not to your coverage of the HSBC but to your appalling coverage of the shocking assassination of Russian opposition leader Boris Nemtsov.

Here was a man who possessed not only courage and principle, but also a girlfriend, one Anna Duritskaya, a 23-year-old model of unparalleled fruitiness. Her omission from Monday's paper I can only put down to the entire red-blooded Telegraph editorial team being replaced by computers! Where were the full-page photos of young Anna, lying on a bear-skin rug, her legs playfully crossed at the ankles while she cheekily necks from a bottle of vodka?

Unless your mighty organ does its time-honoured job, and caters to the needs of my more modest organ, I will have no choice but to cancel my subscription and resort to going online for my "news" requirements.

Herbert Gussett
Old Christopher House, Ogleham.

Mugabe censorship row

by Our Man
in Zimbabwe
Harare Mount

A HUGE row erupted yesterday when it was revealed that Zimbabwe's President Robert Mugabe had prohibited the publication of photographs showing him falling down podium steps.

Mr Mugabe was outraged at the suggestion that he had fallen down, and ordered that all the photographers who had taken the pictures of him falling down should be taken into custody, where, as is common Zimbabwean practice, the police would assist them in falling down flights of steps to their sad and unfortunate death.

"I have never fallen down steps in my life," said Mr Mugabe. "In my country, I leave that to other people."

"Mr Phillips, do you want me to tell your wife again?"

Nursery Times

IS IT THE END OF THE ROAD FOR TOAD?

by Our Motoring Staff **Stig of the Dump-him-now**

CONTROVERSIAL petrol head Mr Toad, was last night in hot water again after a fracas with a weasel in the Wild Wood. Mr Toad had been served up a plate of cold flies, rather than a nice steak and chips, which he'd been expecting.

Toad then allegedly attempted to assault the young weasel. His colleague, Hamster, said, "Toad was hopping mad. He was consumed by Toad Rage. He felt he deserved to be looked after, after a tough day of driving too fast and shouting 'poop poop' at everyone."

Fellow motoring enthusiast Rattarsed, said, "It's all nonsense. Jeremy would never have a fracas, because he hates French food."

Mr Toad, Nurseryland's most popular amphibian, is said to be considering other options, including going to jail for common assault, and then escaping dressed as a washer woman to present a show on Sky, called "Top Women's Gear".

Mr Toad refused to comment, but it is unlikely that he will ever go back to Tony Toad Hall.

On other pages

● Magic Mirror accused of hacking – how it got information on "who's the newsworthiest of them all" **p7**
● Nurseryland government promises 200,000 affordable shoes as starter homes for old women **p22**
● Nick nack paddywack, who gave that dog a poisoned bone? Old Mother Hubbard arrested **p94**

"Eeny, meeny, miny, moe, catch a..."

A Taxi Driver writes

EVERY week a well-known cab driver is invited to comment on an issue of topical importance. This week **A.A. Gill** (Cab No. 666) on the crisis facing TV's Top Gear.

What do you reckon to Clarkson? I mean, what are they thinking about getting rid of him?! Best thing on the telly he is. Diamond geezer! Me and the boys love him. So funny! That one with the Argies. Classic! Just 'cos he's not politically correct. He just calls a spade a spade. And he gets into trouble for that?! I mean, he's the only man in the country who likes to drive a car and tell it like it is. So what if he hit someone. WHACK! Sorry, son. Good luck mending the bike. Bloody lycra Nazis. Nah – the BBC must be mad. I've signed the petition. I had that Enoch Powell in the back of my cab once. Very clever man. Classical scholar. Expert on the works of A.E. Housman. Bit of a racist but nobody's perfect. Oi! Wanker! You blind or something? Oh yeah, sorry – didn't see the dog.

NEXT WEEK: **Reg Dwight** (Cab No. 747) on the alleged homophobia of Messrs. Dolce & Gabbana

That episode you'll never see...

(A middle-aged man with a paunch is driving yet another boring car)

Clarkson *(for it is he)*: Today's Unreasonably-Priced Star in a Fracas is the head honcho, the bee's knees, the dog's bollocks, yes it's me! And I'm in the driving seat of the Mini Fracas, which may sound small but believe you me it packs a hell of a punch. The Fracas is hotter than a cold-meat platter and could cost an eye-watering 150 million pounds – which is almost as much as my weekly salary. I'm not at all happy with the handling and, I'll tell you, the suspension leaves a lot to be desired, but once I put my foot down – bang! – I was gone – faster than a chef clearing off after doing a long day's work. Still, with its state-of-the-art BBC retraction control, a U-turn's not out of the question, especially since the Fracas can get you from nought to 900,000 signatures in under six seconds. With the Fracas, the sky's the limit – and Sky is exactly where I'll be going. And on that bombshell, it's goodbye Auntie Beeb!

(Cue annoying music. And eternal repeats on Dave)

CLARKSON'S LATE DINNER

How about a knuckle sandwich?

News in brief

Highly paid BBC star facing sack after ill-tempered fracas

■ The head of the BBC Trust Ms Rona Airhead, has been threatened with the sack after a tetchy exchange in the House of Commons.

Margaret Hodge apparently presented Rona Airhead with a plate of cold facts about how useless she was at overseeing things, with Rona Airhead insisting that "oversight was her speciality". The argument descended into a slanging match, in which insults were exchanged and such foul language was used that Ms Airhead was eventually offered the job of being the new presenter of Top Gear.
● In next week's Top Gear Rona test drives the new HSBC bullion van. There are lots of laughs as she drives it all the way to the bank.

"Mum! Dad! The Lib Dems are here again..."

ETHELRED THE UNDEAD-Y

R⅁J

NORMAL ED'S KITCHEN

We like a nice night in watching the microwave

Richard III arrested

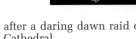

by Our Crime Staff
Hugh Tree

Officers working for Operation Yewtree have confirmed that the bones of Richard III in Leicester Cathedral have been arrested in regard to historic allegations of child abuse.

"The charges relate to the imprisonment and suspected murder of 12-year-old Edward V of England and 9-year-old Richard of Shrewsbury, Duke of York, in the Tower of London in 1483," said Inspector Knacker after a daring dawn raid on the Cathedral.

Inspector Knacker was quick to reject suggestions that, as over five hundred years had passed since the alleged offences were committed, it would be difficult to gain a conviction.

"We're confident that as long as we can dig up some decent witnesses to give evidence against the bones of Richard III, this won't be as big a waste of time as most of the cases we bring."

AN APOLOGY
from the Rt Hon Edward Miliband, Leader of Her Majesty's Opposition

WHEN I said, some years ago, that it was quite wrong for politicians to use their wives and children for the purposes of party propaganda, voters may have been given the impression that I somehow disapproved of party leaders such as Mr David Cameron appearing on teleivsion with members of their family in a cynical attempt to make them look human and to win votes.

I now realise that, whilst it is still despicable and outrageous for Mr Cameron to resort to such cheap and contemptible gimmickery, it is a quite different matter when I do it.

In the modern media environment, it is perfectly acceptable for a respectable party leader, such as myself, to be photographed walking in a park with one's children, or drinking a cup of tea with one's wife in one of the family kitchens.

I would like to apologise for any confusion that may have been caused by my earlier statements on this issue, and I hope that you will find this clarification helpful.

The Alternative Rocky Horror Service Book

HUNTP

**No. 94
A Service for the Solemn Dedication of a New Tourist Attraction in the City of Leicester (as seen on TV)**

The President, the Archbishop of Canterbury (for it is he, although it might be Clare Balding or some other representative of the media): We are gathered together on this historic day to give thanks for the miracle whereby the mortal remains of our former monarch were discovered in a nearby car park and can now be re-interred in this ancient and holy place, to be visited here by millions of tourists from every corner of the world.

Congregation: Too right, bish. Kerching!

President: So let us begin by giving thanks to all those who have made this miracle come to pass. We give thanks to the dedicated scientists of Leicester University who confirmed that these old bones were indeed the genuine article. We give thanks to the bountiful patronage of Channel 4 for its round-the-clock coverage of the events of this historic week here in Leicester instead of their normal afternoon fare, namely the 3.15 at Uttoxeter. And we give thanks that TV's Sherlock is present, solving the mystery of how to boost our ratings.

Benedict Cumberbatch (for it is also he): Elementary, my dear Welby.

President: And, above all, we give thanks that the Almighty should have guided those in authority to choose this previously unknown cathedral in Leicester for the royal re-burial, rather than York Minster, which gets quite enough tourists already.

Congregation: Quite right, Your Holiness, it's time we Leicesterians got a piece of the action.

ADDRESS

(Given by the Dean of Leicester, the Very Rev J.C. Flannel)

Dean: You know, Richard III was, in a very real sense, a complex figure. On the one hand, he was a ruthless tyrant, a mass-murderer and a killer of children. On the other, he was potentially one of our greatest and wisest kings, cruelly maligned by Shakespeare, cut off in his prime and, furthermore, he was disabled. So he ticks all the boxes, particularly for Channel 4, and it is the very fact that he has become such a controversial figure which should ensure that his final resting place will never be short of visitors.

HYMN

(Here the congregation shall sing Hymn 1485)

"There is a gift shop, near at hand,
Within these holy walls.
So get your hands upon your cash,
For now the tea shop calls"

THE DISMISSAL

President: Here endeth the boring bit. Now it is time for you all to pay your respects to the deceased by purchasing souvenirs of this holy day.

(The congregation shall then solemnly process to the aforesaid "Richard III Hospitality Experience", for a refreshing glass of malmsey wine and a plate of lasagne [guaranteed to contain no horse])

Congregation: Let us pay. (Or it may be "I could murder a Little Prince Curry". Or possibly "And one of those Glorious Summer tea towels would be an ideal gift for Auntie Cheryl".)

Lookalikes

Minions

Cameron and Osborne

Halle Berry   **Cliff Richard**

Sir,
    Perhaps some of your readers have wondered about the strange resemblance between the beautiful Academy Award-winning actress, Halle Berry, and the perennially good-looking singer, Cliff Richard? Or maybe they just use the same hair stylist?
    V.P. MALONEY,
Via email.

George Galloway   **Boy George**

Sir,
    While watching news reports of the anti-racism rally in London I was horrified to realise I've never seen Georges O'Dowd and Galloway in the same room. Is there a chance we'll hear "Do you really want to hurt me?" blasting from loudspeakers as the campaign song in Bradford?
    Yours, preferring a cup of tea,
    STEWART WILLY,
Via email.

Corbyn   **Cribbins**

Sir,
    I'd just like to say what a wonderful prospect it is that Bernard Cribbins might be our next Prime Minister. He's left it a little late in life, but then you never get nowhere if you're too hasty.
    TOM YATES,
Via email.

Hitler   **Putin**

Sir,
    The recent portraits to celebrate Vlad Putin's birthday bear a remarkable similarity to the 1933 picture of Hitler as a blacksmith in Wagnerian mode. What is it that makes dictators want to strip off?
    ENA B. RICHMOND,
Via email.

Tea chimp   **Batmanghelidjh**

Sir,
    I'm sure I'm not the only one who has noticed the similarity between Camila Batmanghelidjh of Kids Company and the PG Tips chimp (in Carmen Miranda mode). One makes a good pot of tea, the other makes a good pot of money (untaxed).
    L. KOELLA,
London.

Eddie Hitler   **Paul Nuttall**

Sir,
    I turned on the TV yesterday to see what I thought was an old episode of "Bottom", for there on the screen was the comedy right-wing maniac Eddie Hitler. It was only as the programme moved on I realised I was actually looking at an edition of "Question Time" and the comedy right-wing maniac Paul Nuttall MEP, Deputy Leader of UKIP. I wonder if they might be related in some way? I think we should be told.
    SIMON WASS,
Via email.

Gary Lineker   **Jimmy Hill**

Sir,
    I was wondering if anyone else has noticed that Gary Lineker's chin is slowly morphing into the chin of Jimmy Hill... is this a Match of the Day thing?
    TONY MILES,
Manchester.

David Mellor   **Sir Les Patterson**

Sir,
    I saw in the press this week a photograph of the distinguished former MP, QC, DJ and former Minister of Fun, David Mellor, and found myself thinking of the young, equally distinguished political figure, the Australian Cultural Attache, Sir Les Patterson. Surely they must be related?
    GWEN BRACKET,
Via email.

David Beckham   **Clint Eastwood**

Sir,
    While engaged in some photo research recently, I was struck by the resemblance between these two well-known superstar alpha males. Could they be related in some way? I think we should be told.
    GERRY LYNAS,
Via email.

Father Christmas   **Chuck Blazer**

Sir,
    I love Christmas and am most distressed to see the man I always thought to be my hero all over the media.
    Well, he's not my hero now! I see the FBI have arrested Father Christmas for corruption, working with and colluding with the Swiss Gnomes in Switzerland. What do you think he carries around the world in that big sack of his?
    R. WATTS,
Gloucester.

Mrs Garnett   **Ms Saunders**

Sir,
    Am I the first to notice the similarity between accident-prone Alison Saunders, the head of the DPP, and Dandy Nichols, who played Alf Garnett's much maligned spouse in the TV classic Till Death us do Part? As Ms Saunders has been a silly moo of late over the Greville Janner debacle, I'm sure they must be related.
    JOHN TAYLOR,
Lincoln.

Airship   **Arse**

Sir,
I wonder if any of your readers noticed that the new Airlander 10 airship is hugely analogous to model Kim Kardashian's famous Londonderry Air?

SHEILA MULLON,
London.

French   **American**

Sir,
Is American Gothic the secret to the enormous publishing success that is the psychological thriller-writing couple Nicci French? Readers should be told...

GRANT WOOD (RIP),
Via email.

Henry V   **Clare Balding**

Sir,
While in GCSE English class we noticed the resemblance between Kenneth Branagh as Henry V and Clare Balding.

JOSEPH (age 14),
Salisbury.

Stanley   **Jack**

Sir,
Was that Jack Dee I saw in the next basket to me at the vet's this week?

STANLEY THE CAT,
North Ascot, Berks.

Clangers   **Philae**

Sir,
I noticed a remarkable resemblance between the Philae lander and the spacecraft that landed on the Clangers' home planet and wonder if they are the same?

LAURENCE RICHARDSON,
Via email.

Ed Balls   **Thomas Cromwell**

Sir,
I don't know how Mark Rylance got the part.

JANE O'MAHONEY,
Launceston, Cornwall.

Katie Hopkins   **Proboscis monkey**

Sir,
Perhaps some of your more zoologically-minded readers have noticed the remarkable similarities between the Proboscis Monkey, a member of the Old World primate group, and Katie Hopkins, vigorous proponent of traditional values.

ALEX DUFFIE,
Via email.

Kim Jong-un   **Otto**

Sir,
May I suggest recent events are not the first incursions made into Hollywood by the Supreme Leader.

JEFF FINNEY,
Bangkok.

Hornby   **Pleasence**

Sir,
A remarkable resemblance, Mr Bond.

SIMON ROMPANI,
Brighton.

ET   **IMF**

Sir,
Has anyone noticed, as I have, the similarity between Christine Lagarde and the Extra Terrestrial? The Greek deal is truly out of this world.

JOHN HARRIS,

Statue   **Movie star**

Sir,
At a recent visit to a royal tomb in Geumgok, near Seoul, I was struck by the resemblance of one of the statues there to the actor Donald Sutherland. As is well known, before becoming a celebrated movie star and distinguished pogonophile, Sutherland served during the Korean War as a brilliant if somewhat wayward army surgeon. Perhaps his connections with the country go back even further.

D.G.I. JONES,
Namyangju, South Korea.

Dead   **Boring**

Sir,
Have you noticed the remarkable similarities between Anastasia Steele and the dead smoker on cigarette packet health warnings? Are these two slabs of meat in any way related? They both seem to be having similar amounts of fun. Or is it a case of 50 shades of shadows on me lungs?

TIM STUBBS,
Bristol.

Stephen Hawking   **Austin Powers**

Sir,
A Brief History of Time, baby, yeah!

THOMAS MANSELL,
London, E7.

Non-lookalike

Krankie   **Sturgeon**

Sir,
A number of people have repeatedly and ungenerously likened Nicola Sturgeon to Wee Jimmy Krankie. Can I make it clear that there is no resemblance at all between the Scottish working class hero beloved by millions and the current First Minister of Scotland?

THOMAS FRASER

'We blame police,' say parents of Jihadi schoolgirl brides

by Our Terrorism Staff
Sue E. Sidebomber

The parents of the three East London schoolgirls who ran away to join the Islamic State in Syria said yesterday that the blame for the girls' flight from Britain lay entirely with the Metropolitan Police.

Said one distraught relative, "If the police had done their duty, this tragedy would never have happened.

"Instead of just allowing our girls to be lured out of the country like that, police should have been keeping watch over them 24/7.

"They should have installed secret CCTV cameras in the girls' bedrooms. They should have been monitoring all their emails, Twitter and Facebook messages and they should have hacked into their mobile phones before it was too late.

"It is outrageous that there were not undercover officers in every classroom at the Bethnal Green Academy, dressed in burqas and equipped with secret recording devices.

"Only in this way," the family member who wishes not to be named went on, "could their parents have had any idea what their daughters were up to – and the police should have intervened to arrest the girls at the very first sign that they were planning a secret escape from the country – eg, that all our jewellery had gone missing."

Inspector "Knacker of the Yard" Knacker last night issued a "comprehensive apology" to the families for his force's failure to detect early-onset radicalisation in the would-be Jihadi brides and admitted, "I was not the right man for the job".

FAMOUS FIVE GO TO SYRIA
—by Enid Blyton

"OH, do hurry up, Anne," cried George impatiently. "The boys will be waiting for us to catch our flight. You have been putting that Yashmak on for simply ages."

"I'm ready now," said Anne, standing up beside her cousin. "Let's go and find the boys and we can have a jolly nice adventure as slave brides for ISIS."

The Famous Five had thought of everything. They'd stolen all of Aunt Fanny's precious jewellery and pawned it. Then they'd used that cash to buy ginger beer and plane tickets to Turkey.

This was going to be their most spiffing adventure yet!

"I'm jealous of you two girls," grumbled Jihadist Julian. "When you run away to join the glorious Caliphate you'll be naïve innocents unwittingly lured into ISIS's grasp."

"He's jolly well right, you know," added Dick. "Whereas Julian and I will be pilloried as radicalised teens revelling in the brutality and savagery of ISIS."

"I can't wait to get to Syria and enjoy lashings and lashings of lashings," laughed Anne.

"Just take care not to lose your head," insisted Dick.

(To be continued...)

'NO IFS, NO BUTS,' SAYS CAMERON, 'I GOT THE NUMBERS RIGHT'

by Our Immigration Staff **U.K. Border**

AN unrepentant David Cameron last night hit back at critics who were claiming that he had failed to achieve his target of reducing his number of broken promises to "the low ten thousands".

An official report from the Oxford-based think tank PromiseWatch yesterday revealed that Mr Cameron's Coalition Government has now broken 298,000 promises since it was elected in 2010.

Mr Cameron said, "It is all very well for an unelected think tank to publish alarmist figures about how the whole country is being swamped by our broken promises.

"But we must remember that a great many broken promises are in fact very good for the economy and are helping to build a diverse multi-culture where lies and truth are regarded as of equal value.

Operation Yew Turn

"Merely because I may have said something a few years ago in an election manifesto doesn't mean that there is any excuse for dragging it up again now in an effort to suggest that breaking promises is in some way a bad thing in the Britain of today."

When Mr Cameron was further pressed as to whether anyone should believe a word he says about anything, he offered a robust defence of his entire broken promises record.

Broken promise Britain

"Many of my best friends," he said, "have been broken promises. For instance, I said quite rightly that we would reduce the national debt – and, OK, it happens to have doubled from £700 billion to £1.4 trillion. But no one worries about it. It's just a number. It doesn't mean anything.

"Meanwhile," he concluded, turning slightly pink, "the sun continues to shine, the birds are singing in the trees and I am definitely going off for a really well-earned Easter break in Cornwall.

"And that's one promise, I assure you, that I am going to keep."

'Thin-shaming doesn't work' says The Mail's

Sarah Vain

Trust me. I know. I've been there. Telling people that their columns are a bit thin does *not* make them better. In fact, quite the opposite. Whenever people tell me that my stuff in the Mail is thin, it makes me go out and write an even thinner article. Or two. In fact, I often start binge writing, feasting on thousands and thousands of words *(That's enough, we get the idea, Ed.)*

24/7 Rolling News What You Missed

Man behind desk: And news is just coming in that, tragically, a German airliner has crashed in France, and it seems that none of the 150 passengers is likely to have survived.

Woman behind desk: This is obviously a terrible disaster, and obviously there is a great deal about what has happened that we don't yet know. But we do have on the line an aviation expert who can tell us what to think about what we know so far.

Expert: Well, I'm afraid we really don't know very much yet, except that an airliner has crashed and all the passengers are feared dead.

Man behind desk: I know it's far too early to speculate about what the cause of this dreadful crash might be, but do you think it is likely that it was mechanical failure?

Expert: As you rightly say, it is far too early to speculate, but obviously that cannot be ruled out.

Woman behind desk: Of course, it is too early to speculate, but is there any possibility that there could be some terrorist involvement?

Expert: We simply don't know, but of course at this early stage, terrorist involvement

cannot be ruled out.

Man behind desk: You're watching breaking news and, of course, the main headline is the crash of a German airliner with many people feared dead. The cause of the crash is not yet known, but experts are saying that neither terrorism nor mechanical failure can be discounted.

Expert: Well, we simply don't...

Man behind desk: And, of course, Putin's got some form when it comes to downing passenger jets, so he must be in the frame?

Expert: Er...

Woman behind desk: So it's just coming up to half-past the hour and the main news tonight is of the German airliner that has crashed, killing many passengers...

Man behind desk: And reports are just coming in that contrary to earlier speculation that it was mechanical failure, terrorism, or Russian sabotage, it appears that in fact one of the pilots crashed the plane deliberately. I know it's too early to speculate, but what would cause him to do this?

Expert: As you rightly say, it is far too early to speculate, but...

Man behind desk: It's obviously depression, isn't it?

Woman behind desk: Or gay demons...

Man behind desk: Or an unborn child...

Woman behind desk: Or none of those...

Expert: Well, we simply don't know...

(Cont. on 94 channels)

BBC LETS CLARKSON GO

To be fair, I've been letting myself go for years

OMG! YOU LOOK AMAZING!

HEATH

New BBC show to replace Top Gear

by Our BBC Staff **Ray Tings**

THE BBC's director general, Lord Hall, today announced an exciting new programme to replace the international hit show *Top Gear*.

He said, "We need a new format that will prove to be as successful worldwide as *Top Gear* and will attract both men and women to the channel."

BBC Arts supremo Alan Botney added, "To appeal to the C-D-Es we've come up with an exciting new period vehicle show called *Top Off*, in which Captain Ross Poldark, played by Aidan Turnon, test drives a number of horse and carriages whilst taking his top off.

"There will be blokey banter from a shirtless Poldark and his Cornish cronies as they compare horse power (one) and acceleration (0-4mph in under an hour) and undertake impossible challenges, such as revitalising the Cornish tin-mining industry."

Lord Hall concluded, "In episode one there will be a new feature – Star in a Reasonably Priced Cart – which will have as its first celebrity guest the sizzling cleaning lady, Demelza."

Meanwhile, there are reports that Lord Hall has been the subject of death threats, with angry viewers warning him of "dire consequences" if he attempted to put *Top Gear* back on television.

DRIVETIME
EXCLUSIVE TO ALL RADIO STATIONS

Presenter: You're listening to Drivetime and today's question of the day is: 'Should drivers be allowed to use mobile phones?' I've got Phil on the line. Phil, where are you calling from?

Phil: I'm calling from the fast lane of the M3.

Presenter: Oh right... and what's your view on the subject?

Phil: Well, obviously this is just nanny state nonsense. There's nothing dangerous whatsoever about using your mobile whilst driving, I mean... whooooah!... Fucking hell!... Watch oooooouut!...

(Smashing noise)

(Pause)

Presenter: Thank you, Phil.

Upcoming courses in May

How to be a food critic with Frank Lee O'Bese

This intensive hands-on course will help you foster the illusion that you might one day be paid for stuffing your face. You'll learn everything from eating chips with two hands to spreading mayonnaise on everything to make it taste better.

Tuesday 5 April, 10am-4pm £249

Notworking with Professor of Notworking Julia Hobsbore

Hobsbore, curates a brilliant course on:
● Attracting curated sponsorship for content-free events.
● Curated tweeting every few minutes about how brilliant everything you're involved with i) will be ii) is and iii) was.
● Curating your Notworking globally in a digital age.
● Initiating and curating annual vanity awards for gullible columnists and opinion-formers.
● Inserting the words "curate" and "digital" into all your curated digital output.

24-25 May, £4,500 (plus a curated glass of water)

Pouring money down the plughole with Sir Alan Rubbisher

This hands-on course from veteran Grauniad editor Alan Rubbisher teaches skills that will help you boost your pre-tax losses to £30.6m in a single financial year. You'll learn everything from how to pay yourself up to £395,000 per annum to how to flush your newspaper's resources down the internet.

21-22 May, 10am-4pm, £2,399 (includes sandwich)

Watching paint dry with Mark Grudge

Dealing with all aspects of killing time, this three-day Guardian masterclass covers the basics of staring into space and making another cup of coffee, to more advanced areas of prevarication, such as blaming your parents for everything and lying in bed wondering where it all went wrong.

4-9 May, 10am-5pm £1500

Turning your idea into a prize-binning novel with Sally Slushpile

This rigorous six-month course from globally unpublished author Sally Slushpile includes advice on:
● Starting a novel about your recent break-up with your worthless fucking bastard so-called fucking partner
● Abandoning your new novel after only three chapters
● Downing half a bottle of gin before pressing delete
● Thinking about maybe turning it into a radio play, waiting four months and then deciding against
● Wondering if you might be better off going back to your old job in PR.

May-November £5,495

How to write the same piece more than a thousand times with Polly Toynbee

The basics of everything, from going on and on about how really awful the Conservatives are to going on and on about how really awful the Conservatives are, this course offers a hard-to-follow guide to mixing your metaphors, making your prose duller and boosting your self-righteousness. This inaccessible event from Polly Toynbee will help anyone overcome that perennial problem of trying to write something new. Attendees can give up halfway through.

Wednesday 20 May, 10am-4pm £449

How to make a million pounds overnight with Dave Pauper

This course is for you if...
● You have ever dreamed of making a million pounds overnight.
● You have ever thought of trying to convince someone else they can make a million pounds overnight.
Under the expert guidance of Dave Pauper – high-profile subject of an in-depth investigation by BBC Radio 4's prestigious *You and Yours* – you'll learn everything from how to foster and develop your illusions to the essential components of dipping into your pocket to resource ailing media institutions.

30-31 May, 10am-4pm £729

Forthcoming Grauniad masterclasses for June

● Using the! exclamation mark effectively ● The beginners' guide to writing a beginners' guide ● How to blog about your tweets (including tweeting about your blogs) ● So you want to teach a Grauniad masterclass?

Book now at
thegrauniad.con/masterclarses
(surely some mistake?)

"I'd scrub it out if I were you – stick to your animal paintings"

POP STAR TAKES DRUGS

A POP star was yesterday discovered to be taking drugs. Said a pop star expert, "This is what pop stars do. Particularly when they are young pop stars."

Friends of the pop star commented, "We had no idea he was a pop star. We are now very worried for him." (*Reuters*)

If Modern Buildings Had Accurate Nicknames

THE KNOB — THE PENIS — THE TODGER — THE WILLY — THE OVER-COMPENSATING ARCHITECT

RGJ

Let's Parlez Franglais!

Parte quatre-vingt fourteen Le Vieux Alliance

(Dans le résidence de l'Ambassadeur de France)

L'Ambassadeur: Bienvenue, Madame Sturgeon, le recently elected Ministre Premier de L'Ecosse!

Nicola Sturgeon *(pour c'est her)*: Och aye le nouveau!

(Enter un flunkey avec un pyramide absurd de Ferrero Rocher sur un trai)

Nicola Sturgeon: Ah, Monsieur l'Ambassadeur, vous êtes spoiling us!

L'Ambassadeur: Je regrette que ces chocolates ne sont pas deep-fried.

Nicola Sturgeon: Ah, enough de vos stereotypes culturelles, Monsieur Grenouille!

Ambassadeur Grenouille *(pour c'est lui)*: Ooh la la! Touché, vous êtes très feisty indeed. No wonder que tout le monde parle de Sturgeonmania!

Nicola Sturgeon: Non, non, non. Mais vous êtes dead right.

L'Ambassadeur: Alors, what reckonez-vous de cet election? Trop close à caller, oui?

Nicola Sturgeon: Je ne suis pas wee, Monsieur Grenouille. Je suis plus tall que Jimmy Crankie et aussi votre former Président, Monsieur Sarkozy.

L'Ambassadeur: Tout le monde est plus tall que Sarko, including sa femme fruitée, Carla Bruni!

Tous les deux: Hahahaha.

(C'est un moment d'entente cordiale entre les allies historiques, unis dans leurs contempt pour les Rosbifs)

Nicola Sturgeon: Non, mais sérieusement, nous Ecossais Nationalistes avons une bonne chance de holder la balance de pouvoir, après Mai le septième.

L'Ambassadeur: Sacré bleu! Ou possibly rouge! So, qui fanciez-vous pour le top job? L'étrange Monsieur Milibande ou le nez de toffee Monsieur Cameron?

Nicola Sturgeon: C'est un choix très difficult. Moi, je préfère Alex Salmond à entrer Numéro Dix.

L'Ambassadeur: Hahahahaha!

(C'est un moment d'entente even more cordiale entre les allies historiques, unis par la frite sur l'épaule about les Anglais filthies, untrustworthees, arrogantes, avec leur Agincourt, Flodden, Crecy, Culloden, Waterloo, Twickenham etcetera...)

Nicola Sturgeon: Mais si vous twistez mon arm, je would have à dire que pour les interests d'un Ecosse libre et indépendant, si un peu strapped pour cash, peut-être Cameron c'est l'homme...

Servante civile: Pardonnez-moi, Madame Poisson, could you slow down un peu, je cannot écrire aussi vite pour faire un memo sensationelle et inaccurate, prêt à leaker.

Toutes les autres servantes civiles: Moi aussi.

L'Ambassadeur: Un leak? C'est une légume Welsh! Sûrement, nous n'avons pas room pour une autre stereotype culturelle?

Nicola Sturgeon: Non, non, non, c'est un dirty trick.

L'Ambassadeur: Mon dieu! C'est toujours le même story avec les politiques d'Albion Perfidieux!

Nicola Sturgeon: Och aye the newspapers!

(Fin)

© *The late Kilomètres Kington.*

THE SEAT WHICH COULD DECIDE WHO RUNS BRITAIN AFTER MAY 7

by Our Election Analysis Team

THE sprawling, semi-rural, semi-industrial constituency of Dullton and Snoresworth is the 42nd most marginal seat in the country, and the party which takes it next month will almost certainly be in a position to enter a Coalition to form the next government.

Although Dullton was traditionally a safe Labour or Conservative seat, except when it was run by the SDP in the 1980s, boundary changes have made the seat more unpredictable than ever.

Labour are pinning their hopes on a Snoresworth local councillor, Patsy Postitnote, a former researcher for the trade union Harmony (formerly the Amalgamated Society of Boilermakers).

The Tory standard bearer is Phil Pinstripe, who was parachuted in at the last minute after the former candidate, Ted Teatowel, defected to Ukip, before being exposed by the Snoresworth Echo for having sent a racist tweet to his partner Fiona Filing, the former deputy head of the Council's planning department.

Pinstripe's vote may well be eaten into by the current Ukip candidate, Geoffrey Golfclub, a retired local businessman, although there are signs that the Ukip surge may be fading, following the revelation that Mr Golfclub once shared a platform with Mr Billy Bonkers, a member of the English Defence League, which is not putting up a candidate this time.

The Lib Dems are confident that their candidate, Simon Sandals, will buck the national trend, after his active role in promoting a 2.5 kilometre "cycleway" along the A4273 between the villages of Yawning and Slepe.

The Greens, on the other hand, are sure that much of the previous Lib Dem vote will shift towards their candidate, Wendy Windfarm, a committed writer of letters to the local papers on subjects as varied as climate change, badgers and the need to scrap the monarchy and the armed forces.

A dark horse in the campaign will be the SNP candidate, Hamish McHaggis, although the fact that he is standing for a constituency 300 miles from Scotland might diminish his appeal to a largely Asian electorate.

One thing is certain. No one has the slightest idea what is going to happen in this swing marginal on 7 May and, frankly, nobody cares either.

● Tomorrow in our series focusing on key marginals: Snoreton and Dullsworth.

RESULT FOR TORIES

Hooray! It's not mine

HUSBAND

American Pie

What do those lyrics really mean?

The *Eye*'s Pop and Rock Correspondent, Chevy Levy, analyses the secret meaning behind the song that changed a generation

"American pie" reference to the US branch of the Paedophile Information Exchange, which had infiltrated the civil liberties movement

"helter skelter" rockney rhyming slang for Alka Seltzer, a mind-altering drug used by the Rolling Stones after a particularly loud gig

 **"the jester"** reference to the film *The Court Jester*, starring Danny Kaye, where the Jester sang for the King (played by Cecil Parker) and the soon-to-be Queen (a very young Angela Lansbury)

"the King and Queen" topical conflation of the death of civil rights activist Martin Luther King and the historic state visit of Queen Elizabeth II to Toronto in the year McLean wrote the song

"the quartet practised in the park" the Borodinsky Quartet who famously rehearsed in a Walmart car park in Manhattan before defecting from Russia after the Cuban Missile Crisis.

"Jack be nimble, Jack be quick" the famous call made to Jack Charlton, by Sir Alf Ramsey as Franz Beckenbauer threatened to score in the

1966 World Cup Final, which McLean watched in a bar in New Dworkin, while drinking "whisky and Ribena"

"I was a lonely teenage bronkin' buck" Bronkin Buck was a cowboy cartoon character about whom Buddy Holly wrote the song *That'll be the Day*

 "James Dean" part of the writing duo Pearl and Dean, a pair of Tin Pan Alley Jewish brothers; it was Dean who wrote the lyrics to their famous advertising hit, "papapapah-papapa-papapa", the tune that inspired the young Don McLean to take up the guitar

"while Lenin read a book on Marx" a clever misprint, alluding to John Lennon's adoption of the principles of Groucho Marx, which would eventually split up the Beatles

"Father, Son and Holy Ghost" an ironic reference to the antics of the "rat pack" of Frank "Godfather" Sinatra, "James" Dean Martin and the soon-to-be-ghost Elvis *(Stop writing this drivel or this will be the day your career dies. Ed)*

Foxy Knoxy Found Innocent

by Our Italian Correspondent
Fleet Street Foxy

THERE was widespread dismay in Fleet Street, as editors came to terms with the news that the highest court in Italy had, on appeal, found that Foxy Knoxy wasn't the world's sexiest murderer.

"It seems extraordinary, given how many newspapers she still sells, that the court could have looked at this and found her not foxy in the first degree," said one editor, quietly sobbing.

"If she's not a killer then why is her first name 'Foxy' and not something normal and not murdery at all, like Amanda?" asked another editor.

"Pictures of Foxy Knoxy looking sexy and dangerous are still appealing to my readers," insisted another. "She'll always be guilty of making the hearts of readers beat just a little faster."

Meanwhile, Amanda Knox's parents say they are very relieved that the Italian justice system is such that if you are prepared to have enough retrials you'll eventually be cleared.

"It's a cornerstone of Italian justice that eventually no one is guilty of doing anything."

FOXY FOXY Is he innocent?

BRITISH justice was on trial after the arrest of top DJ Dr Foxy Foxy, accused of *(That's enough, Ed... acting on lawyer's advice)*

"I went for a relaxed fit"

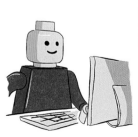   

HILLARY TO RUN FOR PRESIDENT

It's time to have a woman in the Oval Office

Been there, done that

Your Election Questions Answered

Q. I've noticed that none of the parties is talking about foreign policy in this election. Do we have one?

A. Yes, of course we do.

Q. Ok, so can you, for instance, explain where we stand on the Middle East?

A. Oh yes, this is simple. In Iraq we support the fight against the Sunni terrorists or ISIS, which is being led by our gallant Shia allies, the Iranians.

Then in Yemen, we are 100 percent behind our gallant Sunni allies, the Saudis, in trying to crush the Shi-ite terrorists who are acting as a front for the evil Iranians.

In Syria we are not supporting anyone, neither the Shi-ite regime of Assad backed by his gallant Iranian allies, or the Sunni rebels, supported by the evil Saudis. All that's pretty clear, isn't it?

Q. No, you've got me a bit confused there. Are the Iranians our friends or not?

A. The point you're missing here is that by far the most important thing in the Middle East is to stop the gallant Iranians getting nuclear weapons which would stop them being gallant allies and turn them into evil terrorists.

Q. But aren't they pretty evil already, I read that they keep hanging thousands of people?

A. Again you've missed the point. Iran's President Rohani is a "moderate" and a "reformer" which is why he's agreed to give up building nuclear weapons.

Q. Has he really agreed to do that?

A. Well, not exactly. But we're confident that, if we don't mention the hanging and the attempts to overthrow all the Sunni regimes in the region, then one day he probably will, and we shall have lasting peace throughout the Middle East. That sounds a pretty good deal, doesn't it?

Q. No, it sounds completely mad.

A. That's why we don't really want to talk about it.

"Hey, buddy, would you mind stepping out of the vehicle, so I can get a better shot at you?"

The Eye's Controversial New Columnist

The columnist who makes a mountain out of mashed potato

This week I am very angry about the study that shows that babies flinch in the womb when their mother smokes. There may be some so-called "liberal do-gooders" that will take this evidence and claim that smoking while pregnant is a serious health issue, well I utterly refute that and say that so-called "scientists" know nothing and that my Great-Gran smoked twenty a day and lived to 208 and it didn't do her any harm. And the reason why I can muster such brilliantly nonsensical arguments in the face of overwhelming evidence (ensuring my reputation as a top newspaper columnist) is entirely due to the beneficial effects of smoking in the womb. It helped to retard my cognitive functions and discard any trace of rational *(cont. p94)*

POETRY CORNER

In Memoriam Evgeny Lebedev's beard

So. Farewell
Then Evgeny Lebedev's
Beard.

You were very
Funny and made
Us laugh,
Before Comic
Relief spoiled
It all by
Shaving you off.

Now you have
Gone to a
Better place.

Down the
Plughole.

A bit like
Live TV.

E.J. Thribb (17½)
Presenter of Dead TV,
the 24-hour obituary channel

This poem is now on the GCSE syllabus to be memorised by all pupils in Year 11.

THIS WEEK

GEORGE GALLOWAY

Have you got any favourite spoons?

I don't think that's an appropriate question when thirty million Iraqis are lying dead at the hands of Bush and Blair.

Do you like spoons from around the world?

Is this supposed to be some insinuation that I'm anti-Semitic? Is that it?

No, it's just...

This is most unwise of you. You are treading a very dangerous path.

I just meant some foreign spoons are...

I can assure you that I'll be paying you a visit after the election.

That sounds a bit threatening, I only wanted to...

Not a threat, just a promise. You have been most unwise here. Most unwise.

Let's start again. Are there spoon issues in your constituency?

My opponent is a liar. She says she was forced to run away with a spoon aged 15, but I know she was 16. I have reported this to the police.

And has anything amusing ever happened to you in connection with a spoon?

No. And for you to be asking about trivial matters like spoons is an insult to me. You'll be hearing from my lawyers in due course.

NEXT WEEK: *Nicola Sturgeon "Me And My Sturgeon".*

56

The Daily Torygraph

Friday, April 17, 2015

100 businessmen support Tories – shock new letter to Torygraph

by Our Political Staff
Hugh New and **Will I. Never**

IN A dramatic revelation that has rocked the world of Westminster to its core and literally set the 2015 election campaign on fire, 100 rich Tories have written a letter to a Tory newspaper saying that they are Tories.

Seasoned observers have called it the biggest political earthquake since **ever**, pointing out that normally one would expect wealthy Conservative members of the CBI to vote for the Socialist Workers' Party or, at the very least, to back the proto-revolutionary movement led by Russell Brand.

Instead, these affluent leaders of industry have sensationally come out in a letter and signed up to the party that traditionally represents themselves.

This extraordinary turnabout is believed to herald an entirely new era in both national and global political behaviour and the Telegraph has already received two further bombshell letters which it intends to publish later this week.

In the words of the letters editor, these documents will "shatter the status quo and change everything for all time".

In one, a leading pontiff declares himself a supporter of the Catholic church and, in the other, a group of top bears declare their intent to use the woods for the purpose of defecation, come May 2015.

Where will it end, this jaw-dropping sequence of *(cont. p94)*

100 voters sign open letter to businessmen

by Our Election Staff
Poll E. Toynbee

In an open letter to Britain's leading businessmen, a hundred of the country's most ordinary voters have asked them to stop writing open letters to the press warning that a Labour Government would be a disaster for business.

The letter tells the businessmen that the election will be decided by voters making up their own minds rather than being told what to do by a group of self-interested executives whose main concern is what will happen to their shareholders and their salaries.

In the letter, the voters urge the businessmen to shut up and, if their businesses are in so much danger, they should maybe concentrate on running them properly rather than wasting valuable time writing letters to the papers.

The letter, signed by all one hundred voters, concludes that it's a bit rich, these businessmen signing letters, given that they never put their signatures on any letters from their bloody customer service departments.

One small businessman writes open letter to newspaper

■ A Mr Rupert Murdoch has written an open letter to the Sun newspaper this week, which has not been published on the front page. Mr Murdoch apparently said, "Jeezus wept, you bunch of bloody drongos! This race is tighter than a kangaroo's crack and I've got a lot riding on it!

"Why can't you just pitch in and win the election for that useless pommie softball Cameron? He may have a face like a slapped wombat and he may be about as useful as a face flannel in a sandstorm but at least he knows which way my wind is blowing!

"Try a bit harder, you pack of useless bastards, or my business will be even smaller!"

UNFAMILIAR POLITICIAN 'A BREATH OF FRESH AIR'

by Our Political Correspondent **Dave Zhavu**

VOTERS across England were quick to heap praise on Nicola Sturgeon after the seven way leader's debate in which she was declared the winner.

"It's such a breath of fresh air to see a politician who is a real breath of fresh air because we've barely ever laid eyes on them before" said all voters across England. "Nicola's so refreshing compared to tired old faces like Nick Clegg."

Voters were quick to reject suggestions that this was simply a repeat of the 2010 debate, when voters hailed Nick Clegg as a real breath of fresh air because they'd barely ever laid eyes on him before compared to tired old faces like Gordon Brown and *(cont. p94)*

Dave Snooty AND HIS NO PALS

57

FEARS GROW AS ANOTHER YOUNG BRITON TEMPTED ABROAD

by Our TV Staff **Jay Hadi**

SHOCKING footage has come to light of another young Briton who has left the country to join the US ratings war.

The young man, identified as former comedian James Corden, has already been seen in shocking videos all around the world. In one he is seen parading a Hollywood A-lister around before ruthlessly sucking up to him, and cruelly telling atrocious jokes. In another he tortures people with an excruciating song about himself.

Said one former colleague, "Corden used to be Funni, but now he believes fanatically in his own hype. He's dedicated to the cause of making money."

Corden follows in the footsteps of crazed self-publicist Piers Moron, who for many years preached hate in the *Daily Mirror*. Many people are now asking, "Is enough being done by MI5 to make sure these people are never allowed back in the country?"

"Hard hat, hi-vis jacket, farmyard animal and a baby... let's see the bastards top that"

ALL PAPERS

How I Will Vote

by All Columnists

AS a lifelong supporter of the Conservative/Labour/Liberal Democrat party, who has never previously had any doubt as to which way his/her vote should go, I must confess that I have found that this election has confronted me with the most challenging decision of my life.

The dreadful fact is that in recent years, my party has completely lost its way. It has systematically betrayed every principle it once stood for.

We loyal members of the Tory/Labour/Lib Dem party have watched in shocked incomprehension as the party we once knew and loved has turned itself into something that we no longer recognise.

I frankly admit that, like so many others, I no longer have any real idea of what my party stands for.

I have watched in horror how my party leader Mr Cameron/Mr Miliband/Mr Clegg has systematically watered down and compromised every value which once commanded the unhesitating support of millions of ordinary hard-working/hard-working/hard-working Britons.

But at the end of the day, and after prolonged soul-searching, I have finally concluded that, despite my very real misgivings about everything that the present-day Conservative/Labour/Liberal Democrat party has now come to stand for, and despite the dismally lacklustre election campaign run by Mr Cameron/Mr Miliband/Mr Clegg, there is only one way in which any sensible person can possibly cast their vote.

The alternative facing the country, that we might have to suffer the nightmare of being ruled by the appalling Tories/Labourites/Lib Dems, is so unthinkable that I will, with a heavy heart, have no hesitation whatever in voting Conservative/Labour/Liberal Democrat, and I strongly urge every one of you to do the same.

Chilcot Report – New Delay

by Our Procrastination Staff
Anne Otherday

SIR John Chilcot last night announced that his report into the circumstances surrounding the invasion of Iraq in 2003 will now not be published "until all the persons mentioned in it are dead, including myself".

The cause for this latest delay may have been explained by the recent confidential letter sent out by former Cabinet Secretary Sir Jeremy Humphrey to all the 3,512 individuals mentioned by name in the report.

That Letter In Full

Dear ▬▬▬▬ *(name redacted, possibly "Tony")*

I have great pleasure in enclosing a copy of the report on Iraq drafted by Sir John Chilcot and his inquiry team.

When you read it, you will find that it contains a number of references to your own part in the events of 2003, on pages ▬▬▬▬▬ *(page numbers redacted)*.

You may feel that these references are perhaps over-critical of your role, and might appear to you as being somewhat "strong meat".

You may further feel that these references are "unhelpful", particularly where they describe how you " lied through your teeth", "wilfully deceived the House of Commons", "actively conspired to mislead the nation" and "dishonestly led the country into a flagrantly illegal and foolish war, for which you should be tried before the International Court as a war criminal".

If in any way you feel that these references to your actions at that time are not an entirely accurate representation of how you would like to see the history of that unfortunate period recorded for posterity, then of course I will ask Sir John to remove them – under the process known as "Maxwellisation", after that distinguished public figure and philanthropist, the late Sir Robert Maxwell.

I am particularly anxious that we should apply this "right to redact" principle in the case of Sir John's report, because I myself am mentioned in passing in its pages a mere 378 times, due to the fact that, at the time, I was the private secretary to one of the major participants in the Iraq business, a Mr ▬▬▬▬▬ *(name redacted, but believed to be the Rt Hon Tony Blair)*.

I will naturally await your reply with great interest, but urge you not to feel under any particular pressure in this respect, since I have arranged that the final version of Sir John's excellent and comprehensive report will not be published until the 100th anniversary of the Iraqi invasion in March 2003. I consider this to be a much more suitable publication date than the original promised date of 2010.

Yours,
SIR JEREMY HUMPHREY,
10 Downing Street, London SW1.

PS. See you at the Athanaeum for lunch on the ▬▬▬▬▬ *(date redacted)*.

"I had no idea how damaged I'd become until I started saying everything, not once, not twice, but three times"

DIARY

IN OUR
TIME
WITH
MELVYN
BRAGG

MELVYN BRAGG: It's been called one of the most crucial ideas in all human history. But it is also a lot more than that. The concept of EMV, or *equum mortuum verberans* – literally, the flogging of a dead horse – has been around since time immemorial. Consciously or unconsciously, we've all done it – but what exactly does it mean, "flogging a dead horse" and how did it originate?

Charles Darwin, Soren Kierkegaard, Hermes Trismegistus, Baruch Spinoza and Hadron Collider – these are just some of the names that have grappled with this extraordinary theory down the centuries. Yet it is only in recent years that we have been fully able to grasp its profound significance.

With me to discuss the whole question of EMV – in layman's language, that's flogging a dead horse – are Jeff Beardy, Professor of Applied EMV Studies at the University of Queen's College, Oxford; Lynne Nervy, Visiting Fellow in the History of Equine Applications at the University of Surrey; and Gervaise Waffle, Professor of Equine Linguistics at University College, London.

Gervaise Waffle, if I could start with you. EMV is often referred to as a paradigm shift?

PROFESSOR WAFFLE: Oh, very much so. It is, to my mind, a key branch of chaos theory, whereby the sensitive dependence on initial conditions in which a small change in one state of a deterministic nonlinear system can result in large differences in a larger state. So that, if one starts to, as it were, flog a dead horse, then somehow it is in the very nature of the act of flogging to see the continuing process of, as it were, the act of being flogged.

MELVYN BRAGG: You're going to have to say what you mean by that. Let's start with the horse – is it, so to speak, a real horse that we're proposing to flog? Or is it in some way more symbolic?

PROFESSOR WAFFLE: Oh, very much so. At this point, I'd like to backtrack, if I may, and draw your attention to something that we may be in danger of overlooking, namely the human

tendency to backtrack just as things are, as it were, "getting going". But, then again, what exactly do we mean when we say that someone is "getting going"? Are they getting, or are they going, or are they doing something that in some mysterious way transcends both these activities? This is an extremely complex question, by which I mean –

MELVYN BRAGG: Well, we'll come back to that in a moment, if we may. But first I'd like to bring you in, Lynne Nervy. Could I ask you to fill us in – briefly – on the history of flogging a dead horse?

LYNNE NERVY: Well, the story really begins around 650 BC, with major developments in the key years of 43 AD, 706 – and here I'm reverting to the Gregorian calendar for simplicity's sake – 1491, 1542, and to my mind most crucially, 1736.

MELVYN BRAGG: I see. And – just to be clear on this – what was it that, in particular, happened in those crucial years, in overall terms of dead horse flogging? Perhaps you'd expand for us, Lynne?

LYNNE NERVY: Let's stay with those key years for a moment. The history of *equum mortuum verberans* –

MELVYN BRAGG: – that's flogging a dead horse –

LYNNE NERVY: Yes, well the history of EMV –

MELVYN BRAGG: – *equum mortuum verberans* –

LYNNE NERVY: Yes, the history of flogging a dead horse –

MELVYN BRAGG: – known as EMV for short –

LYNNE NERVY: – also contains within itself the parallel histories not only of those horses that, once deceased, are flogged, but also, of course, of those humans who, for whatever reason, and I can think of many, have been driven to the act or practice of flogging those very same late horses. So, if I could start with the first date, 650BC –

MELVYN BRAGG: – and here we're talking a very long time ago, in terms of *equum mortuum verberans* –

LYNNE NERVY – Oh, very much so – well, the year 650 BC is a keynote date because –

MELVYN BRAGG: We're going to have to move on, I'm afraid. Perhaps I could bring you in here, Professor Jeff Beardy. Let's talk about how this discovery of EMV, this idea, fed into the whole notion of man's capacity to, as it were, eke things out, or in other ways protract them, or, in

some sense, draw them out or needlessly prolong them? Just to make it clear: did it perhaps have something to do with the abiding wish to spend an undue amount of time discussing something that would not, in the end, grow any clearer?

LYNNE NERVY: If I could just go back to something I was saying earlier –

MELVYN BRAGG: Well, I hope there'll be time later to go back to what you were saying earlier, but for now, I'd like to put that question to Professor Jeff Beardy. Jeff?

PROFESSOR BEARDY: I'd like to go back to something Professor Waffle said when he talked about the human tendency to "backtrack" just as things were, as he put it, "getting going".

MELVYN BRAGG: I'd like to deal with that a little later, if I may, but for the time being I want to ask something else. Is it significant that the horse is dead? Was it always dead? And would it be equally significant if it were alive? Do you briefly want to come in on this, Jeff Beardy?

PROFESSOR BEARDY: I mean, fundamentally, I wouldn't disagree with that, but, to go back to something Lynne Nervy said a few minutes ago, I would say that the notion of a parallel history in which dead humans are flogged by horses is fundamentally flawed

MELVYN BRAGG: Lynne, you are waving your hand.

LYNNE NERVY: Well, it's not what I said actually, Professor Beardy.

MELVYN BRAGG: Do you want to say what you were saying, Lynnee, or would you prefer to say what you were not saying?

PROFESSOR WAFFLE: Could I just say –

LYNNE NERVY: I'd just say that I didn't say what he said I said, and if I had said what he said I'd said I'd just say that he wouldn't have said that I'd said it.

MELVYN BRAGG: But I don't think that is what he's saying, to be honest. Do you want to recap on what you were saying about what Lynne Nervy said you said she said, Jeff Beardy?

PROFESSOR WAFFLE: Could I just say a few words on String Theory?

MELVYN BRAGG: Well we've ranged from horses to flogging and back again to death, and the part it played in EMV, or flogging dead horses. So I think this would be an excellent time to see if we can expand on Stringing-It-Out Theory. Lynne?

As told to
CRAIG BROWN

MO UNDER SUSPICION

by Our Athletics Staff
Seb Blatter

THE Olympic champion middle-distance runner was last night being linked to a performance-enhancing substance, traces of which were found on his plate during a routine advertisement.

The substance, known in the business as "Quorn", is an extremely unpleasant meat substitute that, if taken in sufficient quantitites, can make

you run very fast to the nearest kebab shop.

The British Athletics Authority has issued a statement confirming that, although Quorn is not technically on the list of banned substances, they could not really recommend anyone to take it.

Meanwhile, Mo Farah refused to comment on claims that Quorn had led to a suspicious injection to his earnings and a huge boost to his performance in the financial field events.

PERCIVAL

"I'm down to my last bullet point"

POETRY CORNER

**In Memoriam
Richie Benaud,
cricket legend**

So. Farewell
Then Richie Benaud,
Unbeaten Australian
Captain and much-loved
TV commentator.

Dust to
Dust. Ashes
To Ashes.

"Morning, everyone,"
That was your
Catchphrase.

"Mourning, everyone."
That is
Ours.

E.J. Thribb (17½,
82½ short of
his century)

ELECTION NEWS

Spouses 'too prominent in campaign'

■ Questions were being asked today whether Samantha Cameron, Miriam Gonzalez Durantez and Justine Miliband were wise to have involved their husbands so heavily in the general election campaign.

"Of course we realise that as David, Nick and Ed are the husbands of such strong powerful women, we'd inevitably at some point see them chopping vegetables in the kitchen and talking about their home life and the children," said one voter.

"But when they started trying to talk about politics it was so embarrassing. They were obviously not media-ready. They should stick to smiling and waving."

THAT AMAZING NICOLA STURGEON MAKEOVER

Then – 1990   **Now – 2015**

The Secret DIARY OF SIR JOHN MAJOR KG aged 77¾

Monday

As the country's leading and most respected elder statesman, I have decided that, in my judgement, I am the only man who can save Britain before it is too late. Oh, yes. That is why I have today arranged to make a very important speech at the prestigious Heckmondwike and Ilkley Moor Bowls Club.

What I have to say will be in no small measure the bombshell that ignites this so far, regrettably, somewhat grey and lacklustre election campaign.

By saying this, I of course mean no disrespect to my successor Mr Cameron, since criticising other Conservative Prime Ministers is the kind of thing that only the ghastly woman whose name I never mention, ie Mrs Thatcher, would do.

Tuesday

I was not at all surprised, when I laid out this morning's newspapers on the breakfast table, to find that my historic speech yesterday has had exactly the electrifying effect on the election campaign that I had anticipated.

My unique point which no one else seems to have noticed was that this new Scottish Nationalist Party apparently wants to destroy the United Kingdom. Oh, yes. Or rather oh, no! As I said to the 12 veteran bowls enthusiasts in front of me in Heckmondwike, "In my day, we destroyed the unions. What Mr Cameron is doing is destroying the Union."

In no way did I wish to be disrespectful of Mr Cameron, but if he was capable of following my example of engaging with real people on real issues instead of sitting around in his posh kitchen pretending to chop vegetables he might have some chance of winning this election. Oh, yes.

I then concluded with a particularly stirring passage, saying, "What this Scottish woman wants to do is to tear apart the country we all love, the England of old ladies drinking warm beer as they fall off their bicycles on the way back from Communion in the evening mists".

There was not a dry eye in the clubroom, as I issued this rallying call to the entire nation. "Wake up, Britain," I concluded, at which, several of my audience did exactly that.

Wednesday

"She really is the most appalling woman," I exclaimed to my wife Norman, as I read the latest front-page stories about this Scottish lady who is apparently going to take over the country, as I warned everyone in my historic speech on Tuesday.

"Well, you would know," replied Norman in what I thought was an unnecessary reference to past events. "You certainly are an expert when it comes to appalling women politicians who get into bed with unsuitable partners and try to break up longstanding unions."

This was neither relevant nor helpful at this hour of need, when the nation is facing its greatest danger since the Maastricht Treaty. Oh, yes.

PRIVATE EYE'S CONTROVERSIAL NEW COLUMNIST

She says the things no one wants to hear!

*Yes, it's...
Katie Kockroach*

I'm sick of all these disgusting columnists trying to get into the gutter with us. We cockroaches have been happily living as parasites, eating shit and spreading filth for centuries and suddenly along come these desperate wannabes invading our territory. I say keep 'em out! At gunpoint if necessary. Don't feel sorry for them. These columnists are better off sinking to new lows(!) and drowning in their own bile. I know that sounds a bit callous and in slightly bad taste, but so what? We cockroaches have got thick skins and I honestly think that come a nuclear war, the only survivors will be *Sun* columnists feeding off human tragedy, blaming the immigrants for everything and *(You're fired, Ed. Be more unpleasant.)*

Daily Mail

COMMENT

Ten things which will happen if Labour gets in

1. The traditional UK greeting of 'hello' will be replaced by the phrase 'see you Jimmy'.
2. All bald people will be forced to wear ginger toupées.
3. Trident will be replaced by the Loch Ness Monster.
4. All men will be forced to wear kilts on their wedding day.
5. Every pub will be required to have antlers above the bar.
6. Fried fish will be given an extra layer of batter and be renamed 'fush'.
7. The weather in the Home Counties will be reduced by ten degrees.
8. Alex Salmond wearing a daft cowboy hat will appear on the new twenty poond note.
9. The head of Nicola Sturgeon will replace that of the Queen on all stamps.
10. Everyone in England will die. *(Is this right? Ed.)*

On other pages

● Relief for many in Nepal as earthquake not as bad as future Labour-SNP government **p.94**.
● Mail publishes UK Witch List – Nicola Sturgeon enters at Number One **p.95**. *(That really is enough of this rubbish, Ed.)*

GNOME MONEY

RELEASING YOUR PENSION POT
YOUR QUESTIONS ANSWERED

Q: I now have a great deal of money. Will that nice man who keeps trying to sell me solar-powered loft extensions want to have a cup of tea with me?
A: Yes.

Q: Will these changes mean I'll be ripped off by conmen?
A: Yes. Your insurance provider will be working alongside the conmen by selling them your details, ensuring that the meagre pension pot you were mis-sold will be emptied rapidly.

Q: My released pension pot is about £100,000. How many cats will that feed a year?
A: Depending on the size and breed of moggie, approximately 800 cats.

Q: I am now sitting on a lump sum of almost half a million. Can I still complain about how hard life is?
A: Yes.

Q: I have advanced dementia. If I spend all the money in my pension and forget about it, can I then re-spend it at a later date?
A: No.

CAMERON IN 'FREE CHILDCARE' PLAN

It's simple, you just leave them down the pub

VOTE LABOUR

OH. OK.

CAMERON GAFFE OVER WHICH TEAM HE SUPPORTS

by our Football Correspondent
Gary Spineker

THE Prime Minister risked losing the entire election with a terrible blunder in a speech about ethnic diversity and sport.

In an off-the-cuff aside, Mr Cameron entirely forgot which was his favourite team, telling the audience that he would prefer them to "support Labour".

This has led to criticism that the Prime Minister has just been pretending to support the Conservative party in order to appeal to the man in the street and that he actually has no real interest in politics at all.

Real fans tend to be passionate about the "beautiful game" of politics and are tribal in their loyalties, whereas Mr Cameron has now given the impression that his interest in the entire business is non-existent.

An embarrassed Prime Minister later told reporters, "I'm terribly sorry. I had a case of Natalie Bennett-style brain fade. What I meant to say is that I am a great fan of Ukip."

Cameron 'lifelong Villa fan'

by Our Political Football Staff
Adrian Chillax

THERE was a new twist last night in the ongoing Villagate scandal that has rocked the worlds of football and Westminster to their very foundation.

The Prime Minister has been accused of being confused about where his allegiances actually lie, but he has now issued a full clarification.

"I am a lifelong Villa fan. Tuscan Villa, Portuguese Villa, Villa in Cornwall. Villa at home, Villa away!

Come on, you Villa! I remember when my dad took me to my first Villa and I thought, 'Yes, this is my spiritual home.' I loved everything about it: the quiet, the lack of crowds and the complete absence of ghastly football anywhere."

Late news

Cameron clarifies: "I am also a West Hampstead fan"

Even later news

Cameron clarifies again: "I know all about the history of my club. Whites was founded in 1693."

Last call!
Any more postal votes?

HUNTER

Grant Shapps

WIKIPEDIA
The Free Encyclopedia

Main page
Contents
Featured content
Current events
Random article
Donate to Wikipedia
Wikipedia store

Interaction
Help
About Wikipedia
Community portal
Recent changes
Contact page

Tools
What links here
Related changes
Upload file
Special pages
Permanent link
Page information
Wikidata item
Cite this page

Print/export
Create a book
Download as PDF
Printable version

Languages
Deutsch
Français
Polski
Русский
Edit links

Grant Shapps (born 14 September 1968) is a British Conservative Party politician. He is co-chairman of the Conservative Party, and incumbent election candidate for Welwyn Hatfield in England.

He is best known for never tampering with his own Wikipedia entry. Whatever else he does, he definitely doesn't do that, no siree.

And if anyone says I do, they'll be hearing from his lawyers, I would imagine. Mr Shapps first landed on the moon under the pseudonym of Michael Green before scoring the winning goal in the 1966 World Cup Final under the name of Geoff Hurst, after which he invented the World Wide Web, but never used his invention to doctor his biographical details on digital encyclopaedias.

Mr Shapps is universally acknowledged as a thoroughly decent, handsome, honest and charming human being [citation needed].

THE DAILY MAIL'S HEARTWARMING 94-PAGE ROYAL BABY SOUVENIR SUPPLEMENT

TOMORROW: Do YOU Think The Mail Should Seek Help And See A Psychiatrist?

Who will be the Godparents?
Those Odds In Full

Princess Eugenix	1-2
Hugo Wight van Mann	4-5
Ribena Calpol-Anstruther-Cough	evens
Floppy or Stroppy Delaverythigne	3-1
Rupert or Rupert Flotsam-Cutzem-Jetsam	7-2
Virginia Branson-Pickle	5-1
The Duke of Earl	8-1
The Earl of Duke	8-1
The Right Honourable Tamara Boomdeeyay	10-1
Velour Parker-Knowles-Shandy-Toppe	15-1
Guy Blotto	20-1
Tiggy Legge-Auvers	25-1
Jolyon St John Wort	28-1
Group Captain Squiffy Squiffington DSO *(RAF Anglesey Search and Rescue)*	66-1
Captain James Hewitt	500-1
Nicholas Witchell	1000-1

Pippa's Second Baby Tips

1 If you're thinking of having a second baby, make sure you've got one already... otherwise it won't be the second, but the first. And don't have two already, because then it'll be the third. I know it sounds complicated, but it really isn't.

2 When the second baby arrives, give it a different name  from the first baby, ie, if the first baby's called George, don't call her George or Georgina. You'd be amazed at the confusion that sort of thing has caused my friends.

3 Baby photos are lovely, so make sure lots of people take photos of your baby. One way to ensure this is to be a member of the royal family. If you aren't already one of these, marry someone who is.

4 You want your child to grow up in a loving environment. So choose its nanny carefully.

5 Nappy care is vital. Look after the second baby's bottom, because when it grows up it could steal the show at its elder sibling's wedding. This will lead to lucrative contracts for columns and publications telling people how to do things, such as in my latest bestselling remaindered book "Egg-Sucking For Grannies".

"...I'M A HUGELY INFLUENTIAL BLOGGER. I'VE BEEN INVOLVED IN SEVERAL SUCCESSFUL POP-UP PROJECTS AND I'M CURRENTLY CROWDFUNDING A VERY EXCITING ARTISAN VENTURE!"

"YEAH. I CAN'T GET A DECENT JOB EITHER."

GRAEME KEYES

Notes&queries

The naming of the Royal baby

● The Rev David Starkey-Raving is quite wrong to claim that the choice of Charlotte as the name for the new Princess harks back to the child's great-great-aunt, the Princess Charlotte von Werthersoriginalberg, the second cousin twice removed of King Frederick "the Mercurial" of Prussia. In fact, the name Charlotte was undoubtedly chosen in honour of the Grand Duchess Carlotta of Meerkatz, the unfortunate wife of the Elector Russelbrandt, who is best remembered for having commissioned a set of six flute sonatas from the composer Telecomm. The Grand Duchess, who was unfortunately tried and convicted of witchcraft after the repeated failure of harvests in Holstein Pilsner in 1713, was the 17th cousin four times removed of Prince Philofax of the Hellenes, the great-great-grand uncle of His Royal Highness the Duke of Edinburgh. It is very touching to think that the new Princess is to be named in honour of her great-grandfather's illustrious 18th-century forebears – yet another example of the Royal Family's unfailing tact and profound sense of history.
Sir Andrew Roberts-Radio, Master of Wellington College, Cambridge.

● I have never read such a load of pretentious rubbish as the claims made by Sir Andrew Roberts-Radio. It should be obvious to anyone with a modicum of commonsense that Charlotte (or "Charlie", as she will be known) has been named in honour of Carole Middleton's favourite uncle, Charlie, who for many years ran a successful second-hand car dealership on the A3741 near Hartley Brewer. Former customers of "Charlie's Motors" will be delighted to think that his name has been immortalised under Royal patronage and will be remembered for many generations to come.
Fred Farage (no relation), Farage's Garages, Thanet.

● None of your correspondents is anywhere near the mark as regards the royal baby's name. Kate Middleton has simply copied the choice of her favourite celebrity, Katie Price (aka Jordan), who called her daughter Princess and *(That's enough of this. Ed.)*

Sarah Vain

On the Royal baby

I had a baby once. Me. Yes, I did. And it was a girl. Incredible. Let me tell you about my labour – not *that* sort of labour because I'm a Conservative like my husband, Mr Vain! Anyway, my baby got stuck and took ages to come out *(What about the Royal baby? Ed.)* and then afterwards I was exhausted and looked a bit of a fright in my old grey Snoopy t-shirt and a pair of faded tracksuit bottoms. *(Any chance of something about the Royal baby? Ed.)* Congratulations to the Duke and Duchess of Cambridge on producing a baby daughter like me. Yes, I did that and I still don't know how I did it, but I did. Yes, me, me, me, me, me, me *(You're fired. Unless your husband is back in government, obviously. Ed.)*

POETRY CORNER

In Celebrationem

Lines on the blessed arrival of Princess Charlotte, daughter to their Royal Highnesses the Duke and Duchess of Cambridge

So. Hullo
Then Charlotte.

This poem to mark
Your birth should have
Been written by
The Poet Laureate,
Ms Carol Ann Duffy.

But she isn't
Interested.
It's time to give
Her the sack.

And I don't mean the
720 bottles of it,
Which should go
To a more
Deserving poet.

El Jerez Thribb (477 litres)

"Did I leave my charger here?"

ROYAL HEIR AND SPARE

Drinks all the time, is up all night and keeps appearing naked

What do you expect? I'm the second child!

How to join the buy-to-let boom

WITH the economy booming, EVERYONE over 55 wants to get into the Buy-to-Let market and make a fortune just as people did in the mid-2000s.

But how do you do it? Just follow our simple step-by-step guide:

■ Cash in your pension pot early and use that money to buy loads of new-build flats off plan, utilising record low interest rates.

■ Watch the value of your property portfolio surge

■ Buy more flats at the top of the market, just as economy starts to tank

■ Watch the value of your portfolio plummet as the housing market crashes, just as it did after the last buy-to-let boom

■ Be forced to remortgage your now largely worthless flats at hugely increased rates

■ Hide behind the sofa as the bailiffs arrive to seize your house

■ Lose everything you own

■ Er…

■ That's it.

YES! THE TORIES ARE BACK

Hands up all those who thought I'd win

PUBLIC VOTE TO KILL MONKEY AND ELECT ORGAN-GRINDER FOR ANOTHER FIVE YEARS

by Our Political Staff **Libby Dem**

IN A surprise outcome to a secret ballot over the musical direction of the country, the general public has overwhelmingly decided to eliminate the monkey and to give the organ-grinder another chance.

Said a spokesman for the public, "We hate these tunes. We've been listening to them for five years and we've had enough.

"We decided it was time to take action.

"It's clearly the monkey's fault and nothing to do with the organ-grinder at all."

The public continued, "If the monkey hadn't been dancing along, we would never have put up with those awful tunes.

"The monkey has paid the price for its slavish collaboration with the organ-grinder.

"We feel a lot better having killed the monkey and look forward to hearing the tunes on their own, without the distraction of a performing pet."

JUBILANT VE DAY CELEBRATIONS SWEEP NATION

by Our Political Staff
David Doodlebug

AFTER five long years, the British public could no longer contain its joy at the news that VE, Victory over Ed, had finally been declared.

Church bells rang, as the entire country took to the streets to celebrate the historic defeat of national socialism and moderate liberalism and the crushing victory of triumphant Conservative leader David Winston Cameron.

Grown pollsters wept openly on television, as pensioners and toddlers alike linked arms with servicemen to sing a rousing chorus of *"Roll out the benefit cuts"*, *"There'll be blue flags over the white cliffs of Dover"* and the youngsters' favourite, *"We"ll tweet again"*.

Mr Cameron gave his trademark V sign to everyone, as he promised "blood, sweat and tears for you and time on the beaches for me".

Mr Cameron said he looked forward to leading the country for "another five, possibly four, years or even three if I get bored".

Her Majesty the Queen joined in the national celebrations, slipping out of Buckingham Palace, with the words "Tell Mr Cameron I'm not in."

Meanwhile, in Whitehall, the festivities concluded with a traditional riot outside Number 10 Downing Street, as an exuberant group of anarchists and SWP members united with the police in a mass brawl, culminating in a moving ceremony of spraying the words "Tory scum" on a cherished monument dedicated to the women of World War Two.

 Dave Snooty AND HIS SHY PALS

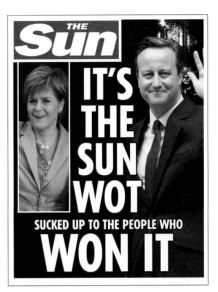

THE TIMES Friday May 9 2015

How tactical voting swung that election

by Our Electoral Analysis Team
Hugh Nose and **Hugh Cares**

AS the results came in, it was obvious to see how the true winners in the election were the sophisticated tactical voters who, in their millions, switched their choice from the party they normally support to a party they cannot stand, in order to keep out the party they really detest.

So in a typical, three-way marginal constituency, such as Snoresbury and Dullston, we can see that the decisive factor on the day was the way Ukip-leaning Lib Dems switched at the last minute to join Labour-leaning Greens to keep out the sitting Conservative, despite the eve-of-poll surge in Green-leaning Labour supporters who joined forces with defecting Ukip-ites and pro-Tory Lib Dems in order to back the SNP who did not have a candidate standing, for the obvious reason that he lived in the Outer Hebrides. Although the outcome, right up to the wire, was too close the call, the *(cont. p94)*

"I suppose I have moved a little to the right over the years"

'Pollsters did superb job' says poll

THE latest survey of a cross-section of the British public indicates overwhelming support for the performance of opinion pollsters during the UK election campaign.

The poll of polls reveals that a staggering 110% of Britons think the pollsters are worth every penny and did either a 'superb' or 'brilliant' job in the run-up to the election.

According to a spokesman for IpsosMoron, "This result has surprised us all. We didn't see that coming. Good grief, are you sure? If that's right, I'll eat my lunch."

ELECTION IN PICTURES

MILIBAND'S MISERY

Cheer up, at least we don't have to pay the mansion tax

MANDELSON'S MESSAGE

Labour needs to stop living in the past …

…and listen to me!

GREEN LEADER'S 'BRAINFADE' SHOCK

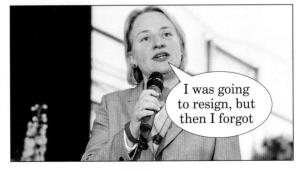

I was going to resign, but then I forgot

KINNOCK JR. TAKES SAFE LABOUR SEAT

I'm allllll right!

MORE HATS THROWN INTO (AND OUT OF) RING AS LABOUR HOPEFULS QUEUE UP TO ATTACK 'USELESS' MILIBAND

by Our Political Staff **Camilla Long-Headline**

THE Labour Party descended even further into turmoil yesterday as seven more Labour MPs of whom no one has heard declared themselves as candidates for the party leadership.

All seven were quick to denounce Ed Miliband as "the worst political leader this country has ever seen".

They all continued, "How anyone could have thought that Miliband should have been chosen for the job is beyond comprehension.

"He never understood that the Labour Party has always been the party of business. It was set up to represent the interests of capitalism and to counter the woeful effects of an over-powerful state.

"We have betrayed the movement by allowing the Tories to steal our policies and to seize the all-important right-of-centre ground, which is where the Labour Party needs to be if it is ever to win another election."

Hunt for New Leader

When questioned about the speeches supportive of Ed Miliband's "inspirational leadership" that all seven of them had been making only three weeks ago, they all replied, "You're taking what I said totally out of context. I only said that Miliband was the real voice of Labour in the context of an election campaign.

"Of course I didn't mean any of it. It was obvious to everyone that Miliband was a totally embarrassing figure who only wanted to drag the party back to the dark days of the Seventies, when the trade union bosses ran the country, rubbish piled up in the streets, corpses were left unburied and giant Marxist rats openly roamed the countryside, eating innocent, hard-working toddlers and their families."

Tristram Hunt is 36.

The Country's Controversial New MP

The columnist who is able to focus on the issues, and certain primary colours

This week I am very happy to be elected as the Member of Parliament for Hoots and Jings Yeken East, incorporating parts of Crivvens. Speaking as a baby *(see photo)* this stunning victory was completely down to me, and not down to the fact I had an SNP rosette on. My constituents know I fought a strong, positive campaign, comprising of several photo opportunities where I kissed the cutest adults I could find.

After watching several episodes of *Balamory*, I was seized by a sudden nationalistic fervour, and was delighted to discover that having spent many of my formative years wrapping myself in a tartan blanket and gurgling, I was more than qualified to stand as a candidate for the SNP *(cont. p94)*

LABOUR IN CRISIS

KEN LIVINGSTONE: I've said this before, in fact I've said this at every election, whether we win or lose. We're simply not left-wing enough. What is clear from this election is that the British public demand a full-blooded socialist agenda and when it's not offered to them, they have no alternative but to vote UKIP.

NEIL KINNOCK: No. I totally and utterly and utterly and totally reject the view, put forward by the public, very publically, in the election, that they utterly and totally and totally and utterly reject the Labour Party, which they don't. What they meant to do was to vote overwhelmingly for a total and utter and utter and total Labour victory of the type I won in Sheffield in 1992. As I said to the public then and I say it now, "You're alllll right (wing, damn your eyes!)".

TONY BLAIR: Hey, who won three elections? Me, me and me! And who didn't? Everyone else! And you know what the difference was? Me! Which suggests the need for a real reassessment of Labour Party policy. It's either me, or you end up with the Tories – which is the same thing. That'll be £2,400 plus VAT. Cheers!

ALASTAIR CAMPBELL: This Government is not legitimate. They're all bastards. The public were scared by the right-wing press into a stupid decision, instead of being scared by me into the right one. Now fuck off, I've got a fucking kilt to eat.

"I can't believe Labour didn't win. We tweeted, we Facebooked and Instagrammed. Perhaps we should have voted"

POETRY CORNER

In Memoriam Christopher Lee

So. Farewell
Then Christopher Lee.
Yes, you were Dracula.

You were 93 when
You died,
Or was it 473?
Now you are out
For the Count.

But are you really dead?
Keith says we should
Put a stake through
Your heart just
To make sure.

The sun has finally
Set on your
Distinguished career,
So we'll see you up
And about very soon.

E.J. Thribb (Cert 17½)

The Adventures of Mr Milibean

Fountain & Jamieson

HEIR OF SORROWS
A Short Story Special

by Dame Sylvie Krin, author of
Duchess of Hearts & *You're Never Too Old*

THE STORY SO FAR: Charles' attempts to influence national policy by writing letters to government ministers have been cruelly exposed by the newspapers. Now read on…

"TAKE a letter, Sir Alan," commanded the Prince of Wales, as he sat steaming in the ornate, cast iron roll-top beignoir made by the old Victorian firm of Farage & Carswell in 1878.

Sir Alan Fitztightly, the Beadle of the Bathroom Royale, sighed, as he expertly applied his organic loofah to the tense shoulders of the heir to the throne.

"Are you sure you wouldn't rather just lie back and relax, sire?" soothed Sir Alan, as he sprinkled a handful of Duchy Original Invigorating Marquess-of-Bath Salts into the troubled waters surrounding the soaking Soon-To-Be-Sovereign.

"No, no," replied Charles testily. "How dare they interfere with my… er…"

"Interfering, sire?" queried Sir Alan.

"No, I prefer to think of it as… er…"

"Meddling, sire?"

Again the aide-de-campingitup unhelpfully finished his master's sentence.

"You're missing the whole point of the thingie, Sir Alan. As a future monarch, one has to be engaged in matters of national importance, and so on."

"Quite so, sire," agreed Sir Alan, as he poured a minute tincture of Nicholas Witchhazel Homeopathic Herbal Balmy into the swirling, pungent liquid mixture, upon which floated a rubber novelty Patagonian Tooth Fish. Perhaps that would help to calm his fretful Fief-Lord.

"I have decided there is only one way to stop people criticising my letters and that is to write a letter to the Prime Minister."

"I expect it'll be a stiff one," smirked Fitztightly, "as Backstairs Billy used to say to the under-footman when he woke him up in the morning in the dear old days of your Nan…"

"Yes, thank you, Sir Alan." Charles upbraided his equerry-as-folk for his ribald reminiscences of times past and snapped, "Could you get on with taking down this letter?"

"Of course, sire, I'll just get my quill out and dip it in, as Billy also said to the over-valet of the…"

Charles cut him off abruptly and began to dictate:

Dear Sir,
It really is appalling.
You remain my humble servant,
Charles, Rex in Attendens Longorum."

Sir Alan wrote down the angry words and then passed the A4 vellum parchment for Charles to sign with his favourite Nosey Parker Pen. The Prince scribbled his signature in his trademark black, spidery hand.

"*Now* can we relax, sire?" asked Sir Alan, filing the letter carefully in the wastepaper bin. "Perhaps a little light music on your marvellous wind-up wireless device?"

Sir Alan cranked up the Trevor Baileys Ethical Cream Radio and turned the dial to the Classic FM Bathtime Show.

But instead of the soothing sound of relaxing Rachmaninov played by the Julian Lloyd-Fellowes Quartet came the voice of cultural commentator Claudia Winkelfringe.

"And the big London news is of course that the Queen has been replaced by a younger monarch, heralding a new era in…"

Sir Alan realised instantly what was about to happen, but before he could turn off the radio's theatre round-up Charles had leapt from the bath and was sprinting down the corridors of Highgrove shouting, "Eureka! It's finally happened! She's gone!" Then he crashed through the doors of the Tracey Emin Drawing Room, to the surprise of his consort Camilla, who was entertaining the ladies of the Jam-Making Committee of the Middleton-in-the-Wold Islamic Women's Institute.

Charles' noble face turned the same shade of red as the halal strawberry

preserve, as Camilla greeted him with the words, "Hello Chazza. We were just debating whether Kristin Scott Thomas will make a better Queen than Helen Mirren in that play. What do you think?"

Charles thought that if this sort of misunderstanding *kept* happening, he would have no option but to write an angry letter to the radio…

(To be continued…)

Paxman calls for end to BBC licence fee

by Our Media Staff
Phil Screen

In an interview with himself, the former Newsnight presenter Jeremy Paxman claimed that the £145-a-year BBC licence fee was "no longer sustainable".

When questioned by himself as to why he had changed his views on this matter, Paxman explained, "The whole broadcasting landscape has changed, making a rethink essential.

"Of course there was a time," he told himself, "when it was perfectly right and proper for the Corporation to collect this revenue to fund its vital public service broadcasting."

Paxman, however, refused to let himself off the hook over why it was no longer acceptable for the BBC to collect £3 billion a year from its audience.

Turning on himself, he repeated the question 14 times in a row: "What has actually changed, Jeremy?"

Eventually, Paxman blurted out the answer that his remorseless interrogator had been determined to extract from him.

"OK, Jeremy, I admit it," he wept. "The BBC no longer needs all that money because it is no longer paying my salary."

Jeremy Paxman is on Channel 4.

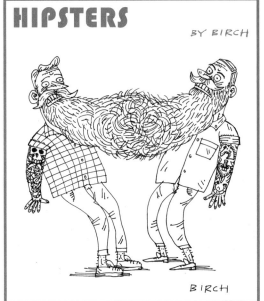

BLATTER PROTESTS INNOCENCE

My hands are clean!

GAOL!

GRAEME KEYES

"This is so much more enjoyable than football"

grizelda

FIFA LATEST

⚽ FOOTBALL ROUND-UP

Footballers praised

Three Leicester City footballers have been praised for reminding everyone there's more to football than just FIFA corruption, as they indulged in a racist orgy with prostitutes whilst on an end-of-year trip to Thailand.

"Football has always been about more than bribing your way to being awarded the world cup," insisted a spokesman for the FA.

"It's about indulging the vices of grossly overpaid idiots because they can kick a ball around a bit.

"Thankfully, this trio's disgraceful antics have reminded us of the true meaning of football."

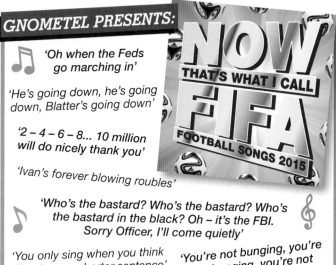
MODERN NURSERY RHYMES

Little Jack Warner
Sat in the corner,
With a finger in every pie.

A surprise lay in store,
There's a knock at his door –
Oh, look! It's the FBI!

THE Sun SAYS

The Bootyful Game

The recent FIFA revelations have shocked us all. We can be in no doubt that money has corrupted the beautiful game.

And much of the blame for the money ruining the game can be traced back to one man, a man who even in his dotage appears to rule his fiefdom unquestioned and unchallenged, the titular head of an organisation mired in allegations of illegal payments.

And that is why we say the time has come for NewsCorp boss Rupert Murdoch to (*You're fired, Ed.*)

Who do you want to succeed Sepp Blatter as President of FIFA?

| Robert Mugabe | Vladimir Putin | Lutfur Rahman | Len McCluskey | Simon Cowell | Don Corleone | Kim Jong-un | Sepp Blatter again |

Simply cast your vote then throw it in the bin because a Qatari will win!

Cameron admits pre-election promise 'hard to deliver'

by Our Political Staff
Philippa Column *(soon to be head of Number 10 Policy Unit)*

In a forthright and wide-ranging tweet last night, the prime minister admitted that when, before the election, he had promised voters "the Earth", he had perhaps underestimated the difficulties of actually delivering the Earth.

"Don't get me wrong," he twittered, "I am already involved in tough negotiations with all the various people we will have to get on board if I am to deliver the Earth. I am speaking to Mr Juncker, Mrs Merkel, the British Medical Association, the judges of the European Court of Human Rights, the Pre-School Care Providers' Association, the Head of the Inland Revenue and even my colleague George Osborne.

"They have all been making it clear to me that delivering the Earth might not be quite as easy as some people have suggested – and I can see that getting agreement on some aspects of my Earth programme may take a bit longer than the commentators might like."

In a further tweet, Mr Cameron explained, "It's not like the old days when, if I promised the Earth and didn't deliver, I could always just blame the Liberal Democrats."

Westminster insiders were last night indicating that Mr Cameron's toughest task could be convincing Chancellor Osborne to pay for all his promises, on the grounds that to do so would "literally cost the Earth".

> NEW JEANS?
>
> NO, NEW CAT.

HOW GOVERNMENT POLICY WORKS Pt. 94

Social Housing

Affordable Housing

Empty Super-Rich Investment Housing

CRIME OF THE CENTURY

HEIST THIEVES NOT ARRESTED

by Our Man in the City **Bob 'Rob' Diamond**

IN WHAT has been described as the most daring and audacious theft of the modern era, a group of professional bankers from RBS, Barclays, JP Morgan and others got away with billions of pounds of other people's money without going to jail.

Details of their sophisticated bank raid have now come to light and observers have been amazed at the amount of coordination, planning and downright greed which lay behind their massive criminal undertaking.

Describing themselves as "the three musketeers", the "Cartel" and average representatives of the "banking community", they carried out the robbery on their own clients over the course of a couple of years, using high-tech methods such as lying and stealing and then covering it up.

However, the gang have now been rumbled and face years not in prison as they are not arrested and not tried and not sentenced.

Said one, "It's an incredibly fair cop. He hasn't even named us." The banker continued, "The fines are fairly hefty, but we're not paying anyway, hahahahahaha." He then continued to laugh, all the way back to his place of employment.

The police remain keen to talk to no one in connection with the crime that they are already calling "too complicated to understand".

ECONOMIC NEWS

UK PRODUCTION 'GOES THROUGH CELLAR'

Government trumpets latest low economic figures

How did Britain achieve this economic miracle?
By keeping crucial financial indicators LOW...

✓ **Low pay & investment**
✓ **Low staff training levels**
✓ **Low management skills**
✓ **Low government-led infrastructure plans**

> HAVE A GOOD EVENING
>
> OR FUCK OFF AND DIE

Balanced news coverage

Russia celebrates Eurovision success

by Our Man in Vienna **Graham Naughty**

You have successfully cast your vote for Sweden

RUSSIA was today celebrating after millions of late phone votes meant it finished second to Sweden in the Eurovision song contest.

"At the half-way point in the voting, when Russia was ahead, it looked as if the most homophobic country on earth was going to be hosting the most flamboyantly homosexual event on the planet," said one Russian official.

"Thankfully, millions of last- minute votes from a phone line inside the Kremlin pushed us back into second place.

"I thought her range was as impressive as my missiles," said President Putin, congratulating the Russian singer Polina Gagarina on coming second. "This is the only time I'm happy for Russia to be defeated in a battle with another European country."

Greek offering

In a dramatic, last-minute bid to stave off bankruptcy, Greece has offered its 81 Eurovision points to its creditors.

"After raiding the banks, pension companies and the petty cash tin over the past month, this is all we have left to offer them," said Greek Prime Minister Alexis Tsipras.

UK flop

The UK's Eurovision entry, David Cameron, flopped spectacularly as he was awarded nul points from other European leaders at the EU Summit in Riga.

"They don't appreciate my Euro Vision or my attempts at petty point scoring," said Cameron after he finished singing his mournful Euro ballad *We're Off*.

"He wants us to dance to his tune. Surely the UK knows by now that isn't the way Europe works?" said lead judge Jean Claude Juncker.

ISIS Threatens Historic City

by Our Political Staff **Jihadi Jon Snow**

How it will look: city in ruins

FEARS were growing amongst historians and archaeologists last night that the terrorist group known as ISIS or Islamic State was about to take over the historic capital city of London and destroy its unique heritage.

The success of the ISIS fighters on the ground has meant that they are now poised to seize control of the ancient city known to the Romans as Londinium and to vandalise its most valued landmarks.

London is a treasure trove of architectural marvels dating from the earliest civilisations to the glories of the London Eye and the O2 Arena.

Said popular Islamic historian Tom Holland-Park-School, "If you think of St Paul's Cathedral, Westminster Abbey, the Houses of Parliament, the Tower of London and Madame Tussauds, you can see that the jihadists would have a field day destroying targets that they consider idolatrous.

"It is time that the world woke up to the danger of ISIS and put the whole of London inside the British Museum where it will be safe."

In the Theatre at Palmyra

"Sorry... it's gone... what's my motivation again?!"

Notes & queries

Is this a portrait of Shakespeare?

● I cannot believe the Reverend Pilbrow has fallen for this one. The idea that the elegant bearded young man in the frontispiece to the 1597 edition of *The Gardener's World* by Montague Don is William Shakespeare is completely ludicrous.

The good reverend has read the clues entirely wrongly, mistaking a willow for a reference to "William" and a wobbly spear for the surname of the Bard, ie Shakey Spear.

In fact, the young man is standing not next to a willow, but in a boggy field or "marsh". And behind him you can clearly see a small bird, a tit or, to use the Tudor vernacular, "a titch".

Add this to the fact that the spear is nothing of the sort but in fact "a lance" held by a nobleman and you have a solution so simple that I'm surprised the Reverend Pilbrow could not see it.

"Sir" "A lance" "titch" "marsh" – who else would be gracing Mr Don's almanac but that distinguished herbalist and man of letters, Sir Alan Titchmarsh?

Professor MCC Newman, Lords.

'I did not lie,' lies Coulson

by Our Political Staff
Michael White-Lie

AS he walked away from court, a free man (for once), lying jailbird Andy Coulson took the opportunity to tell the reporters some home untruths. "I was cleared of lying," he lied, "and I haven't just been let off on a technicality about perjury."

He continued fallaciously, "This trial has completely vindicated my reputation as someone whose lies aren't always important. I can go home with my head held low, and look in the mirror, or indeed the Sun, and say 'I did nothing right'."

Mr Coulson called his trial "a waste of public money". This was a remarkable statement, as – given the trial failed to get him locked up again – it was actually true.

Mr Coulson's reputation was established after some years as a Wapping Liar, and he went on to become a high-flying fibber as David Cameron's Head of False Communications.

Mr Coulson has denied he is writing a book about his experiences. It will be out next year.

POETRY CORNER

**In Memoriam
Charles Kennedy,
1959-2015**

So. Farewell
Then Charles Kennedy,
Decent, likeable,
Principled, funny,
Yet somehow
A politician.

You led Britain's
Third party before
They became
The fourth.

A man of great
Spirit. Though,
Alas, in the end,
Too much of it.

Cheers.

E.J. Thribbute (17½)

Those Kennedy Articles In Full

*"The Charles Kennedy
I knew"* by most hacks

*"The Charles Kennedy
I didn't know"* by most
other hacks

*"The Charles Kennedy
I can't remember if I knew
or not"* by hacks who
drank even more than
Charles Kennedy

*"The Charles Kennedy
who knew me"* by all
politicians

*"The Alastair Campbell
I knew"* by Alastair
Campbell

(That's enough of this. Ed.)

Alex Salmond A BOOK OF TRIBUTES

*Buy the new book by MP Alex Salmond, where he pays
tribute to the great figures of the last 400 years!*

Charles Kennedy
A great fellow, and a sincere personal admirer of the entire Scottish Independence project. Despite his actively campaigning, speaking and urging everyone to vote "No" in the referendum, I always detected a note of sarcasm in his tone of voice. I'm confident that in his heart of hearts he was willing us to win.

Margaret Thatcher
"Margaret", of course – or "Meg", as she preferred to be known – was desperate for Scottish independence, and only didn't say so publicly because of the difficulty it would have caused with her party. And did I detect in the blue of her dresses the same blue that flutters proudly on the Saltire? I think I did.

Winston Churchill
A man, of course, who loved nothing more than to invoke the "Scottish Lion" in his speeches, drinking his trademark whisky all the while. Who can forget his stirring words to the British nation during its darkest hour, "We shall fight them on the beaches of Arbroath, we shall fight them over the proposed cuts to the Barnett formula"? Not me, that's for sure.

William Shakespeare
Shakespeare, famously, wrote many plays about Scotland, including *Macbeth, The Two Gentlemen of Dunfermline, A Midsummer Night's Dram*, and *Much Ado About Full Fiscal Autonomy. (That's enough. Ed.)*

Cameron Pledges To Deal With Immigration Using 'Every Means At His Disposal'

by Our Border Control Staff
Phil Country

THE Prime Minister has sworn that he will use every method available to him to slash net immigrant numbers.

"In reality, of course, there are almost no methods that are available to me, so I do admit that actually 'every method at my disposal' consists of going around politely asking Eastern Europeans if they wouldn't mind not coming here," the Prime Minister said, adding "And

actually, I don't mind terribly if they do come here."

The Prime Minister went on, "But I do intend to go for a lovely holiday in Tuscany with Sam and the kids, so that's already brought the net figure down by five, and frankly I think that's actually pretty good of me.

"If everyone just did that, we could sort this whole problem out at a stroke."

*"There's another one
sneaking into
the country!"*

A Taxi Driver writes

EVERY week a well-known cab driver is invited to comment on an issue of topical importance. This week **SID ROADRAGE** (Cab No. 6742) on the London Mayor's intervention in the debate about taxi cab regulation.

God, did you see that Boris Johnson on his bicycle? I didn't, 'cos I'm a taxi driver. One minute you're driving along complaining to an empty back seat about Uber nicking all your business, the next you're shouting at the bloody Mayor of London on his bike, and giving him a traditional "hand signal" (if you get my drift). Then he has the bloody nerve to get all uppity and tells you to "f*** off and die". What a wanker! As I think I may have indicated at the time. With language like that he should step down as Mayor straightaway – and become a cabbie. Now where was I? No idea – I should work for Uber. I had that Andrew Mitchell in the back of my cab once. Reversed into his bike. Hahaha.

71

HEIR OF SORROWS
A Short Story Special
by Dame Sylvie Krin, author of *Duchess of Hearts* & *You're Never Too Old*

THE STORY SO FAR: Prince Charles has decided to join Twitter, the social networking phenomenon, to keep him in touch with his subjects. Now read on...

"I'M not sure the bath is the best place for this, sire," worried Sir Alan Fitztightly, Charles' aide-de-very camp and Silver-Surfer-in-Waiting, as he watched Charles tapping at the keyboard of his gold-cased onePhone, a present from the Sheikh of Fifah.

"Oh, stop being such an old fogey, Sir Alan," said Charles testily, as he lounged in the foaming waters of Organic Jojomoyes Bath Balm, with just his royal head and noble thumbs above the surface. "This is the future, this is how the world communicates... you see, I can say anything in 140 words." Sir Alan sighed. "I believe it's 140 characters, sire."

"Really?" Charles sat up in surprise, creating a mini-tsunami which overturned his model King Charles aircraft carrier, sending it to the murky bottom of his original Burnham & Kendall Victorian hip-bath. "It can't be done! I'm almost halfway through and all I've written is 'words don't often fail me, but when I consider this architectural outrage, I have to say it really is...'"

Sir Alan had the awful feeling that this new experiment with social media was doomed from the very beginning. "Might I suggest you use an emoticon, sire? They are very economical and cover a full range of emotions, including 'happy face' 'angry face'..."

"What about 'appalled face'"? Charles interjected. Sir Alan was struggling for a reply when Charles suddenly noticed something on his phone.

"Look! I've received my first tweetie-thingy from this marvellous girl I've been following on the BBC Urdu service – Ahmen Korma, I think her name is."

The experienced footman braced himself for the inevitable. "And what does Ms Korma have to say for herself, sire?" Sir Alan glanced over to see on the screen the words "Queen Elizabrth has died @BBCWorld" – but it was already too late. A full-blown tsunami of water cascaded across the bathroom and down the spiral staircase as an exuberant Prince Charles leapt from the bath. "It's the BBC! This time it must be true! Smiley face, smiley face, smiley face!"

As the naked figure of the heir apparent cartwheeled down the corridor under the disapproving gaze of a wall-mounted stag, Sir Alan retrieved the discarded telephonic device from its watery grave and poured cold water on it to remove the foam, a process he would soon have to repeat yet again with his over-excited Monarch-Still-in-Waiting.

(To be continued...)

PUBLIC FOOLED BY COWELL FAKE

by Our Rover Reporters
Henri Matisse, Chevvy Chase and **Skippy the Bush Kangaroo**

THE nation was outraged as it came to light that people had been hoodwinked into watching what they thought was an original programme, but it turned out to be an almost exact double of another talent show.

One, calling itself *Britain's Got Talent*, entertained the public and extracted millions of pounds in phone votes, but all along it was nothing but a clever copy of *The X Factor'*

A furious public complained to OfCom: "How were we supposed to know that this show featuring desperate wannabes with sob stories about dying relatives and a panel of alternately encouraging and bitchy judges was exactly the same as the other programme featuring desperate judges, sob stories about dying wannabes and a panel of..." *(Is this right? Ed.)*

Simon Cowell said, "If you are unhappy about what you were watching, then call this number: 07979797979. Calls will be charged at premium rates of 25p a second."

On other pages
● Is Simon Cowell's tan fake? **9**
● Does Simon Cowell's moob have a double? **94**

Nursery Times
.... Friday, Once-upon-a-time ....

MARY POPPINS DENIES THEFT

By Our Domestic Staff
Jim Jimminy, Jim Jimminy and Jim 'Jim' Jeree

THIS week, the highest court in Nurseryland has seen the trial of super nanny Mary Poppins who stands accused of stealing from the Investment-Banks family.

The prosecution told the court how Poppins was apprehended trying to fly away with a magic bag full of items of jewellery, credit cards, a laptop, an iPad, a Mercedes car and a kite.

Poppins had mysteriously appeared in answer to an advert posted by the Investment-Banks children.

After going on her alleged thieving spree, Poppins was arrested and interviewed by Superintendant "Super" Califragilisticexpialidocious.

A witness for the defence, a chimney sweep named Burt, told the court "Meery Pourpins is not Goilty". He was promptly sentenced to six months of elocution lessons.

Poppins also stands accused of setting the Investment-Banks children on a path to obesity by feeding them a spoonful of sugar.

(The case continues...)

On other pages:
● Distance-running Gingerbread man in doping scandal **37**
● Fifa-Fi-Fo-Fum giant forced to give up goose that lays golden eggs **56**
● Old woman who swallowed a fly goes to Dignitas – expect she'll die **97**

Whatever the British say, he was a great man!

![Andrew Roberts photo and Napoleon portrait]

Napoleon Bonaparte writes exclusively for the Eye on the truth behind the myth of Andrew Roberts

AT only 5 foot 4 inches tall, and with a vaulting ambition, it has long been only too easy for the British to caricature Andrew Roberts as a vain, ego-driven poseur who has rightly been written off as someone who was fatally taken in by his own inflated notions of his role in history.

We are all familiar with the stories of how Roberts liked to hob-nob with all the great and good of his time: such as his dinners at the White House and his tête-à-têtes with press lords such as Conrad Black and Viscount Rothermere.

Everybody remembers the famous incident where he claimed to have been miraculously saved from death by drowning by no less a figure than the future prime minister of England, David Cameron.

All this has added up to a deeply unattractive picture of a ruthless, self-promoting little megalomanic who deserved nothing but ridicule.

But I, Napoleon Bonaparte, having considered the evidence, can now exclusively reveal to the world that everyone has got Mr Roberts terribly wrong.

In fact we can only marvel at the way, as a young man, he appeared from nowhere and within a short time was being recognised as the most brilliant historian of his age.

He so towered above his admiring contemporaries that he dominated the world of history like a colossus.

For years, just as I myself did in my own more modest way, he moved effortlessly from triumph to triumph, sweeping all before him. One after another, the other major historians of his time crumbled before the unstoppable force of his unique genius. Who now remembers Antony Beevor, Max Hastings or Niall Ferguson?

In the end, none of them could compete with Roberts's incomparable skill at dashing off a "Why, oh why" piece about Winston Churchill for the Daily Mail here, or a Spectator Notebook revealing to the world how he had been a fêted guest at the New Dworkin Festival of Bonapartist Studies or a television documentary revealing that Hitler was a secret Nazi.

After such a dazzling career, he made in the end only one tragic and fatal mistake.

He published a book about myself, so silly that it can only be described as his Waterloo.

The Mail ON SUNDAY
····· JUNE 21, 2015 ·····

'ALL MEN ARE PAEDOS' SHOCK

by Our Paedo Staff
Peter File

A SHOCKING new report by the National Paedophile Agency has today revealed that a staggering 100 percent of men in Britain are on-line 24/7, trawling the net for paedo-related material.

The devastating report claims that the entire male population of Britain should be arrested immediately and charged with paedo crimes before being locked up for ever.

The report goes on to demonstrate that all Britons are living less than 6 feet away from a paedo and that anyone showing signs of being a paedo, ie being male, should be reported to the police at once, unless, of course, the police turn out to be paedos as well, which is more than likely, given that everyone is.

The National Paedophile Agency has now demanded a huge reallocation of resources to combat what they call "a paedo tsunami" which is threatening to engulf the whole of Britain in a giant tidal wave of Paedo Mania!

Happy Father's Day!

© *The Pervy Male on Sunday.*

In the Mail tomorrow

■ Junk Mail to swamp Britain – outcry as thousands of copies of the Daily Mail are delivered to people's houses.

PRINCE GEORGE LEARNS FAST

And what do you do?

"Did you read that about gulls becoming more aggressive?"

HOW THE EYE COVERED WATERLOO AT THE TIME

PRIVATE EYE

This'll sort out Europe, once and for all

MADAME GLENDA
■ Phwoar!! That Napoleon, eh??!! "Not tonight, Josephine?" It would be "Yes, tonight, Glenda!!!" if Boney (geddit??!!) fancied coming round to my salon!?!?"

DAVID SPARTACUS
(Leader of the Pro-Jacobin Revolutionary Alliance of Neasden)

Er, basically, until Britain embraces the concepts of total Liberty, utter Fraternity and, er, utterly total Equality, we will always be at the mercy of an aristo-capitalist hegemonic elite who are sickeningly committed to suppressing the working *(cont. volume 94)*

A Hansom Cab Driver Writes

BLIMEY, Guv! That Waterloo, eh? Good thing the Germans turned up! You can always rely on the Hun in a scrap against the Frogs! I 'ad that Duke of Wellington in the back of the cab once. Very clever military tactician...

GREECE APPEALS TO EU OVER DEBT

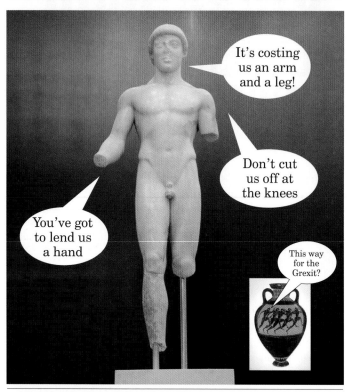

It's costing us an arm and a leg!

Don't cut us off at the knees

You've got to lend us a hand

This way for the Grexit?

GREECE ON BRINK OF BEING ON BRINK OF BRINK

by Our Economics Correspondent **Robert Pestonandonandonandonandon**

THE WORLD held its breath last night as Greece teetered on the edge of the endgame in the last chance saloon as the make-or-break whistle was blown and the final curtain descended to mark the very end of the road leading to the...

All right, I've no idea what's going to happen and nor has anyone else.

GREECE IN NEW CRISIS

GREECE faced a new disaster this week, as it emerged the country is toiling under an enormous shortfall in metaphors to describe the country's situation.

"We've used absolutely everything," said one anguished headline-writer. "We've done 'Greek tragedy' thirty or forty times, we've done the one about them losing their marbles, we did 'Greeks bearing gifts', we did 'Greece! The Musical'. We even had a go at one called 'Elbow Greece'. But we may have to face facts. We can't carry on like this if things keep getting worse there every single day."

Those technical financial terms in full

Grexit
Greek exit from Eurozone
Brexit
British exit from the European Union
Grextremelyboring
Readers exit from the article at the thought of reading another piece about Greek debt.

What You Missed
Dragon's Den
BBC2

Fruity blonde: My money-making scheme is to have an affair with you and then sell my story to the highest bidder.
Dragon: How much are you looking for?
Fruity blonde: About £25,000.
Dragon: I'm in – all the Sunday papers.

Exclusive to Private Eye

Cameron's Top Secret EU Wish List

by Our Political Editor
Brussell Brand

IT IS the best-kept secret in British politics – what is Prime Minister Cameron actually planning to demand in his negotiations with the EU for that "new relationship" between Britain and Brussels, which he intends to put before the electorate in an In/Out referendum in 2017?

So far, he has kept his cards very close to his chest, but now Private Eye has obtained a top-secret document, hand-written on the back of an envelope and found in the dustbin of a Cornish holiday home.

That shock list of Britain's non-negotiable red-line demands in full

1. Britain must take back the power to design her own telephone boxes.

2. Britain must take back the power to decide whether or not to have weekly bin collections AND to choose the colours of the relevant bins.

3. Britain must take back the power to call fizzy white wine made in Kent "champagne" if it jolly well wishes. And if that's too much to ask, then maybe we can at least call it "Fake Champagne-style British Prosecco".

4. Britain must be allowed to retain the right for vehicles to drive on the left-hand side of the road THROUGHOUT THE UNITED KINGDOM (with the exception of Scotland).

5. Britain must be permitted to retain the right to put the portrait of Her Majesty the Queen on postage stamps without prior consultation with Mrs Merkel.

6. Britain must be given the right for her fishermen to catch the single European fish left in her waters.

7. Er... *(That's enough Cameron demands for "major reform of the EU". Ed.)*

"Oh come on – someone must remember how to set up a junta!"

POETRY CORNER

Lines on the retirement of Alan Rusbridger

So. Fraewell
Thon Alan Rubbisher,
Oditor of the
Grauniad.
(That's enough typos. Ed)

Lines on the retirement of Alan Rusbridger, written with aid of spellcheck

So. Farewell
Then Alan Rusbridger,
Editor of the
Guardian for the
Past 20 years.

You oversaw the
Smooth transition from
Broadsheet to website,
From print to digital,
From profit to loss.

"Ich bin ein
Berliner Press",
That was your
Catchphrase.

Now you have gone
Upstairs to a better
Place (the boardroom),
Where you will
Continue to live
In a cloud.

E.J. Thribb (17½ readers)

Isle of Ely, 1071

Hereward – are you a wake?

THE GREEK VOTE: WHAT DOES IT MEAN FOR THE UK?

Your Questions Answered

Q I bought a tea-towel when I went to Crete last year. Can I still use it to dry the dishes?

A It depends. Larger tea-towels can only be used if they are decorated with columns or vases. Smaller tea-towels with bunches of grapes and donkeys are no longer acceptable, and should be cut up for dusters.

Q I am a big fan of Vangelis. Can I still listen to my 'Chariots of Fire' CD?

A No. All Vangelis soundtracks are now outside the official EU preferred easy listening playlists. You may hand in your CDs at your local HMV where they will be exchanged for 'Conchita Wurst sings Serge Gainsbourg' or a box set of German oompah music.

Q My parents brought me a bottle of something from Lesbos. It's blue, and it's been in the back of the pantry for eight years because it tastes like lighter fluid. What should I do with it?

A The government of Greece will be repatriating all their blue drinks over the next few months, to aid in further negotiations. Please place in a waterproof box by your door so they can be collected by an unshaven man carrying a spade.

'Why weren't the churchgoers armed?' asks NRA

by Our U.S. Staff
Charles Town

FOLLOWING yet another tragic shooting in America, representatives from the NRA have pointed out that if only the church had been fitted with a well-stocked firearms cabinet, the entire tragedy could have been avoided.

"It's plain to see that more guns are the only solution to the problem of madmen with guns," said board member Hank Glocktoter. "If this church had had a security guard, maybe an Iraq veteran, who had a big gun and free licence to shoot anyone he thought looked dodgy, then this dreadful event might have been prevented.

"The fact that it wasn't speaks volumes about the sad state of America today."

Those NRA recommendations in full

- Bibles to be fitted with small, single-shot Derringers as standard
- Prayer cushions contain space for a hand grenade
- Crucifix can easily be made from two crossed bazookas
- Pews "long enough to get a sniper rifle under"
- Pulpit to be adapted into small, easily-sealed machine-gun nest
- All worshippers to have two guns sellotaped to their hands at all times
- More guns. More guns. More guns. More *(That's enough guns. Ed)*

HOW RUSSELL BRAND SEES HIMSELF

HOW OTHER PEOPLE SEE HIM

APPARENTLY THEY COME INTO HOUSES TO FIND A MATE

ALRIGHT, BARRY? PINT?

Royston

The Timons of Athens

Friday 10 July 2015 BC

TSISIPRAS DEFAULTS ON BOULDER ROLLING OBLIGATION

BY OUR TRAGEDY AND COMEDY CORRESPONDENTS
HUGH RIPIDES AND
HARRY STOPHANES

THE Greek leader Tsisipras has announced he has no intention of completing the task of rolling the massive weight of debt up the hill.

"What is the point? It only comes rolling back down again. And to make it worse, every day the rock gets bigger."

Civilians living at the bottom of the hill are concerned that they will be flattened if Tsisipras gives

up the task set for him by the Gods, Mrs Merkel and the EU-Menides – known as the Furies due to their anger at the thought of not getting their money back.

King Pyrrhus welcomes referendum victory

KING Pyrrhus of Epirus today hailed the no vote in the Greek referendum, describing it as a stunning victory for Syriza.

"This result was in the face of overwhelming odds reminds me of my stunning victories defeating the Romans at Heraclea and Asculum."

King Pyrrhus continued, "Both battles won spectacularly at only the minor cost of my forces suffering irreplaceable casulties.

"I have no doubt that Syriza's referendum win will go down in history as being every bit as pyrrhic as my victories."

Queues form outside Horn of Plenty

THERE were long queues of angry pensioners outside the fabled Horn of Plenty last week. The Cornucopia had been shut for a week and was failing to provide any grain, milk, grapes, or even wine, to waiting customers.

One pensioner, Jason, 35, complained, "I've been fleeced." He went on to explain, "You come along here to this hole in the horn, and expect plenty of abundance. And what do you get? Austerity! It's outrageous!" Said another elderly citizen, Tiresias, 378, "It's a disgrace. I never saw this coming. They're robbing me blind!"

(Stories to be repeated for the rest of time).

75

WIMBLEDON PICK OF THE TOURNAMENT

The Eye's choice of the top-performing swearers in this year's championship

EFFI BLINDER, 27
Potty-mouthed US star who proved that she is as good at swearing on grass as she is on clay

YURI SONOVABITCH, 31
The Ukrainian with the big mouth and booming voice you can hear all over the court

FUK YU, 23
Exciting Chinese challenger who has served up an impressive volley of abuse

HUGH WANKER, 20
British bad boy who swore at an incredible 190 decibels per hour

SHAVI TUPYURAZ, 27
Indo-Czech newcomer with a powerful range of shits

JESUS H CHRIST, 33
Veteran American blasphemer who could go all the way to being banned for ever

Wimbledon is sponsored by Robinsons Soapy Water – perfect for washing your mouth out!

A Doctor's Locum Writes

AS A locum doctor, I'm often asked, "Doctor, would you like £460,000 a year?". The simple answer is "Yes, please".

What happens is that the NHS is suffering from a complaint known as Chronic Shortstaffing and experiences a condition called *In locum dependens*, to give it the full Latin name.

This requires an emergency procedure in which the locum in question grabs the management by the testicles and squeezes them until money starts to flow.

When an obscene sum has been yielded, the operation is declared a success and the locum goes to the bank, leaving his account very much healthier.

If you are worried about the NHS haemorrhaging money on temporary staff, you are **quite** right!

© A Locum *(column written for the Doctor at a cost of £46,000 per word).*

"You should concrete over. Makes life so much easier"

From The Message Boards

Members of the online community respond to the major issues of the day...

Children's party cost £2,500

Please, please join my Facebook group REAL PARTIES FOR REAL KIDS! and put an end to "birthday party inflation". The average cost is now hundreds of pounds, as parents compete to provide increasingly lavish entertainments, and some themed parties cost as much as £100,000! Most shocking of all was Sarah-May Dickson boasting of spending £2,500 on her daughter's fifth birthday party, despite the fact that she's an unemployed single mum living in Canvey Island. **– Supermum**

fives a bit young to be a mum, even in essex! lolz! **– hatfield gooner**

I see she named her daughter Princess Bliss, which tells you everything about this ghastly woman. **– Araminta**

not bein funny but is the name princess so bad? even kates copyin the idea callin her boy prince gorge short for prince gorgeus? **– Hayley 321**

People ask how this woman can afford it, but what about the cost to the environment of all this consumption: can our PLANET afford it? Instead of baby showers and parties, we had a Sustainable Shower and a Fairtrade Fun Day, with no presents and no "party food". The children drank water (the most precious gift on Earth) and foraged for nettles and berries. In place of the dreaded goody bags they each got a biodegradable carrier bag full of rubbish, with instructions for an interesting recycling game to play at home. **– Emily**

I agree about educating through play. As a World War Two re-enactor, recently promoted to the rank of SS-Gruppenführer, I have run numerous Nazi-themed children's parties (or Jugend Rallyes, as we call them). It's a great way to broaden their minds and challenge negative stereotypes about Germans. I also agree with the fine blonde woman from Essex that giving children aspirational names can boost their confidence and self-esteem. My son is called Übermensch (Übi for short). **– Legion of the Damned**

We held a traditional party for our grandchildren, with coconut cobbles, jam sporrans, liquorice stools, fish paste crusties, suet stumps, pork clinkers and Welsh eggs (Scotch eggs with tripe instead of sausagemeat). All washed down with mutton tea, brewed with proper mutton bags! A blind boy won "pin the tail on the donkey", which seemed unfair because he had an advantage, so we gave the prize to the runner-up. The only unfortunate moment was when our dog bit the magician's rabbit. **– Jennifer Smith**

bite the magicians rabbit, is that a euphemism? **– Danny Daz**

No, why? **– Jennifer Smith**

comedian's say is that a euphemism on panel games, its kinda random. havent you heard of it? **– Danny Daz**

No. **– Jennifer Smith**

D I A R Y

MICHAEL PORTILLO'S GREAT BRITISH RAILWAY JOURNEYS

Portillo stares out of train window

PORTILLO (voice over): In 1840, one man transformed travel in the British Isles. His name was George Bradshaw and his railway guides inspired the Victorians to take to the tracks. Now, 170 years later, I'm following in his footsteps, being filmed getting on and off trains, walking in a straight line along platforms, and showing how extraordinarily interested I can be in what ordinary people have to say.

PORTILLO: I'm now almost three quarters of the way through my journey from Barchester to Borchester via Burchester to Berchester. One of the reasons I enjoy visiting this part of the country is to be reminded quite how many truly dull parts of this country there are.
(pretends to leaf through Bradshaw's)
They were, it seems, every bit as dull in Bradshaw's day. And none duller, it would seem, than Burchester. Time now, though, to find out how the good folk of Burchester pronounce the name of their home town!
(turns to fellow passenger)
PORTILLO: Excuse me interrupting you, ordinary local, but do you hail from Burchester?

MAN IN SMOCK: Maybe I do, maybe I dint.

PORTILLO: Wonderful! So perhaps you could enlighten me: should one pronounce it Berk-hester, or Burch-ester?

MAN IN SMOCK: BERK.

PORTILLO: *(alighting from train in his pink jacket)* Well, the jury is still out on that, but I'm greatly looking forward to finding out what goes on in this most exceptionally uneventful of old English market towns!

PORTILLO *(pretending to flick through Bradshaw's)*: In Bradshaw's day, Burchester was renowned for its truly mediocre stuff. Victorian visitors to Burchester would be sure to drop in on the town museum, home to a fabulously unremarkable collection of local gubbins. It all makes me anxious to learn more. Hello! You must be Fiona, the museum curator!

FIONA: Yes, Michael.

PORTILLO: And, looking round, I'd say this must be one of the most truly unexceptional collections of this and that in the British Isles!

FIONA: For centuries now, Michael, the Burchester townsfolk have prided themselves on their ability to gather objects of little or no signifance under the same roof.

PORTILLO: Ah! This looks like a flint to me!

FIONA: Yes, it's one of over 2,000 in the collection, Michael. And the extraordinary thing is that they're all roughly the same.

PORTILLO: So what exactly would the good people of Burchester have done with these flints, Fiona?

FIONA: They'd pick them up – and then put them down.

PORTILLO: And I understand you're going to give me a lesson in how to pick up a flint!

FIONA: Yes, Michael. So you just pick it up.

PORTILLO: Like this?

FIONA: Yes, Michael. And then you put it down.

PORTILLO: Like this?

FIONA: Yes, Michael.

MICHAEL: Brilliant! And what would this flint have been called in your great-great grandfather's day, Fiona?

FIONA: A flint, Michael.

MICHAEL: So just the same as it is today. Well, isn't that extraordinary?

PORTILLO: Having been schooled in the time-honoured tradition of picking up and putting down an old flint, I've now moved on to a muddy field on the outskirts of Burchester. You must be Jim!

JIM: Yes.

PORTILLO: So tell me what it's like to stand in a muddy field, Jim. A bit muddy, I imagine!

JIM: Tha's right. Bit muddy.

PORTILLO: And this mud – I've noticed that if you walk into it wearing a nice clean pair of new wellington boots in a pastel shade, it soon sticks to them, and makes them go all muddy, too. Why exactly is this, Jim? Perhaps you'd talk us through the whole muddy-making process?

JIM: Well, you walk into the mud, and then all that mud gets your boots all muddy.

PORTILLO: And this mud consists of – what exactly?

JIM: Mud.

PORTILLO: Mud! And what's the technical word you'd use describe it?

JIM: Muddy.

PORTILLO: On my next journey, I'll be following Bradshaw to see for myself the first collection of buckets in Boreham-on-Tweed, I'll be hearing of the tragic event in 1891 when the town carnival was postponed for a few days owing to a sudden shower of rain, – and I'll be hearing from someone called Steve about the ancient old art of filling up schedules in the early evening.
(exit Portillo on a train)

As told to
CRAIG BROWN

MIGRANT FLOOD WORRIES HOME OFFICE

by Our Political Staff
Peter O'Border

THE Home Secretary, Mrs Theresa May, called for tighter controls on UK borders, as the latest flood of migrants swarmed out of Britain, heading for the Middle East.

"The numbers are getting out of hand," she admitted, as an astonishing twelve people slipped through Customs to begin a new life not in the United Kingdom.

Said Mrs May, "They clearly believe there is a better life in the war zones of the Third World and they are willing to risk everything to get away from Dewsbury."

A spokesman for ISIS, the international terrorist organisation, said, "All these Brits are coming over here and taking our jobs as fighters, brides, suicide bombers, etc. It's great!".

"You look different, have you had some work done?"

77

Cameron points finger of blame for Tunisian massacre

by Our Political Staff **Peter Nomore**

THE world of Westminster was rocked to its foundations last night when Prime Minister David Cameron laid the blame for the recent deaths of British holidaymakers in Tunisia firmly at his own door.

"I must come clean about this," he said. "The gunman on the beach was trained in Libya, which is now one of the central breeding grounds for terrorism in the world.

"If I hadn't sent in the bombers in 2011 to destabilise that country there is a very good chance that the firm rule of Mr Gaddafi would still be keeping the country free from these Islamicist lunatics who train people to go back to Tunisia to kill innocent British holidaymakers.

"I have no doubt that I should be put on trial for war crimes along, of course, with my friend and role model, Tony Blair."

EXCLUSIVE TO ALL NEWS CHANNELS

TUNISIAN HORROR
Those Interviews In Full

Phil Airtime: And now we have exclusively managed to track down Walter and Iris Wetherspoon who are prepared to tell us for the first time about their harrowing involvement in the Tunisian holiday massacre that has stunned the entire world – or at least Britain. We've got Walter and Iris on the line now, to talk us through what they went through on that terrible morning when a lone gunman cold-bloodedly shot down 38 innocent holidaymakers, most of whom were British.

(We see grainy picture of Mr and Mrs Wetherspoon taken at their daughter's wedding ten years ago, followed by stock footage of loungers on beach)

Phil Airtime *(puts on grave face)***:** Walter, let me come to you first. Can we ask you to relive those painful and terrifying hours when you got caught up in a nightmare that you can never have expected when you and your wife booked your holiday of a lifetime only four months ago?

Walter: Yes, well, we were not actually in the hotel where it all happened, but we were in one nearby, only a mile or two away.

Iris: And we'd decided not to go to the beach that morning – not the actual beach where it happened, but another one which was nearer the supermarket.

Airtime: And so where were you in the middle of a terrible tragedy?

Walter: Well, we did hear some noises which we thought might have been a car back-firing, but we didn't think anything of it until we watched the BBC News in our bedroom later.

Airtime *(puts on an even graver face)***:** That must have been a terrible shock for you, to realise that you were at the heart of a major international tragedy. I know it's difficult for you, but could you describe what your feelings were at that moment?

Iris: Well, obviously, we were very surprised and sad, and we were very sorry for all those poor people who'd lost their lives.

Airtime: And did you immediately contact your tour company to demand that you should be flown home to Britain on the next flight?

Walter: Oh no, we thought we might as well finish our holiday since we'd paid for it and we're still here.

Airtime: Thank you very much, Walter and Iris, for that incredibly moving first-hand account of what you went through only five days ago.

Philippa Slott: Phil, that was extraordinary. Could you tell our viewers what your feelings were as you listened to that remarkable testimony?

Phil *(eyes welling with tears)***:** Well, Philippa, it's hard to put it into words but *(Cont. for 94 hours on all channels)*.

"I'm taking a selfie of myself taking a selfie!"

KenPyne

TUNISIAN BEACH SELFIE SHOCK

I need to get the perfect shot

What should we call ISIL?

THE GREAT DEBATE
YOU CHOOSE

THE Prime Minister has told us that we should no longer refer to the Middle Eastern terrorist group as the Islamic State because it is neither Islamic nor a state. So what should we call this bunch of murderous psychopaths instead?

a) the "So-Called Islamic So-Called State" (SCISCS)

b) the "Islamicist Non-State of Iraq, the Levant and Dewsbury" (INSITLAD)

c) DAESH (Death to All Europeans Seeking Holidays)

d) a "very small minority of radicalised extremists who have no connection with the peaceloving religion of Islam" (VSMREWNCPRI)

e) That crazy death cult that's just like the new Mad Max film where they all shout "Valhallah-akbar" as they blow themselves up (MM)

f) SPW (Sir Peregrine Worsthorne)

(That's enough alternative names for Isis, Ed.)

DAVID CAMERON LEADS ONE-MINUTE SILENCE

What are you going to do about ISIS?

VERY LATE NEWSFLASH

PRIME MINISTER OBJECTS TO MEDIA USE OF ENEMY NAME

MR WINSTON Churchill last night called upon the BBC to stop calling Adolf Hitler's bunch of fanatical extremists by their chosen name of 'Nazis'.

Churchill said, "The so-called National Socialist party are neither Nationalists nor Socialists. After all Mr Hitler is hardly leftwing. And he is not representative of his nation as a whole. So we should call him, and his death cult, what they are – Nasties." The Prime Minister then went off for a much needed holiday to Churchillax and cut the defence budget *(is this right, Ed?)*.

78

LABOUR LEADERSHIP CONTROVERSIAL FRONT-RUNNER EMERGES

by Our Political Staff **Michael Whitehair**

THE LABOUR party is on the brink of electing as leader a left-wing firebrand who has the support of the unions and is determined to take the party away from the safe middle ground of politics and into the radical extremes.

Whilst supporters of Andy Burnham and Liz Kendall look on with dismay, there is no doubt that the late Michael Foot looks set to become the next leader of the Labour Party.

"The fact that Michael Foot has been dead for years," said one enthusiastic supporter, "should not deter us from making him our next leader. I think his donkey jacket and walking stick could be the trademarks of a new modern Britain and

that Michael will lead us into a bright new past."

He continued, "Michael is the man to take Britain into the 1970s. And one thing is for sure, the voters won't say 'he's too left-wing for us. Let's keep the Tories in power for a decade'."

A spokesman for the trade union UNIGHTMARE said, "People didn't vote for Ed Miliband because they thought he was too right-wing and anti-union. The late Michael Foot ticks all the boxes, including the one he is buried in. He is the one to pull off a 2020 election defeat, as he is the ultimate symbol of the current Labour Party, being dead."

Jeremy Corbyn is 66.

Everyone suddenly remembers what Tories are like

by Our Political Correspondent **Ann Kneesia**

PEOPLE across Britain have belatedly remembered exactly what it is they voted for in May.

Many people voted for the Conservatives under the impression that they were, "you know, those nice ones, who are a pretty safe pair of hands". Others recalled dimly from before 1997 that "we can

trust them not to ruin everything".

Now, with the NHS under attack, the BBC on the verge of being sold off, the courts being closed down, schools being turned into academies, people having benefits cut unless they can prove they were born before 1935, and Grant Shapps back in government, people have suddenly remembered, "Oh, it's THOSE Tories we just elected!"

'CHECK SCHOOLS FOR FUTURE TERRORISTS'
by Our Education Staff **Brian Wash**

DAVID Cameron has insisted that school heads should look out for pupils being groomed by extremists.

"We all know now that every young man involved in one of these heinous acts of terrorism is described by their family as being a sweet, kind and generous kid, the sort of

person who wouldn't harm a fly, who loved sport and reading and was popular and had lots of friends.

"If head teachers see any of their pupils displaying any of these tell-tale signs of radicalisation they must report them immediately to the security services."

BUDGET FOR INHERITANCE

I'm going to inherit your job!

Nursery Times

································ Friday, Once-upon-a-time ································

BUDGET SPECIAL

by Our Economics Staff **Mary Mary Quite Contrary Riddell**

SO how does Georgie Porgie's emergency budget affect you? Across Nurseryland we look at the Winners and Losers.

Loser
Footwear-dwelling pensioner
With the cap on child benefit limited to two children, the old woman who lives in a shoe will not have sufficient broth let alone bread to feed her extended family. "I don't know what to do," said the old woman who lived in a shoe.

Winner
House-builder's Son
The house that Jack built will now be inherited without any financial penalty by his son. Jack's legacy of the house will be tax-free and will include the dog that worried the cat that killed the rat that ate the malt that lay in the £1 million pound house that Jack built.

Loser
Non-Dom and Etonian Pirate
Captain Hook lives in offshore Neverland,

thus avoiding paying tax in Nurseryland. He will now have to choose between his domicile in fashionable Mermaid Lagoon and his Pirate HQ located in the City of London.

Winner
Senior Aristocratic Military Officer
With the defence budget guaranteed to rise in accordance with the NATO (Nurseryland Armed Toys Organisation) target, the Grand Old Duke of York is a surprise budget beneficiary. After years of cuts he is to receive 10,000 new drones which he can fly to the top of the hill and down again and which are much cheaper than actual "men".

The Rest of the Winners and Losers

Losers	Winners
Tinker	Rich man
Tailor	Thief
Soldier	*(That's enough.*
Sailor	*Ed)*
Poor man	
Beggar man	

SAVING FOR HAT

How the Queen's Nazi photo was covered in the press

BY NEWS INTERNATIONAL PAPERS

THE TIMES

A clearly not-bothered Queen laughs off Nazi picture

The Sun

IT WAS THE SUN WOT HUN IT! HER MAJ PRAISES SUPER SOARAWAY ROYAL SCOOP!!!

BY NON-NEWS INTERNATIONAL PAPERS

The Daily Telegraph

Queen appalled by scoop which turns out not to be a scoop at all and it was rubbish by the way

Daily Mirror

TEARFUL LIZ ON 24-HOUR SUICIDE WATCH AFTER NAZI STORM

Daily Mail

WHY WE WOULD NEVER PUBLISH THESE SHAMEFUL PICTURES, AS THERE'S EVERY CHANCE VISCOUNT ROTHERMERE TOOK THEM. WHOOPS!

ROYAL FAMILY SALUTES EDWARD VIII

Hands up if you think I'm a Nazi

ROYALS GREET HITLER

Have you come far right?

HARRY COMFORTS QUEEN IN NAZI ROW

Just tell them you were pissed

HEIR APPARENT 'TOO YOUNG TO HAVE UNDERSTOOD'

NOT EXCLUSIVE TO THE SUN

by Our Royal Staff
Queen Elizabeth Murdoch

THOSE close to James Murdoch have expressed their revulsion at the publication of highly embarrassing images showing him sitting next to Rupert Murdoch, thought to have been taken at a Select Committee hearing at the House of Commons in July 2011.

"You have to remember that James was only a mere child of 40 when these photos were taken, meaning he could have had no understanding of just how evil

News Corp was," insisted close associate Rebekah Brooks.

"Little James was simply mimicking the gestures of his dad when Rupert said 'no comment' whenever he was asked what he knew about phone hacking."

London Underground Offers New Service
THE PICKET LINE

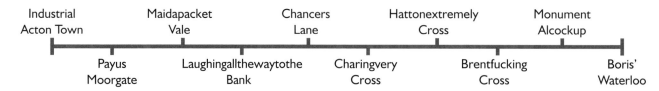

Industrial Acton Town — Maidapacket Vale — Chancers Lane — Hattonextremely Cross — Monument Alcockup

Payus Moorgate — Laughingallthewaytothe Bank — Charingvery Cross — Brentfucking Cross — Boris' Waterloo

EU Leaders Reach Historic Deal Over Greece

by Our Political Staff
Andrew Marrbles

AFTER 48 hours of continuous negotiation, the EU's heads of government and finance ministers emerged triumphantly this morning to announce that they had finally resolved the long-running crisis over Greece and the rest of the eurozone.

The agreement, reached at 4.30 this morning, after some of the "toughest talking the EU has ever known", was hailed by Mrs Angela Merkel as "a great day for Europe".

"We have agreed to destroy Greece," she said. "We have persuaded the Greeks to allow their country to be destroyed, which was their original objection to our bail-out terms.

"The terms were previously 'callous', 'unforgiving', and 'impossible', but after negotiations, we have amended them to 'impossible', 'unforgiving' and 'callous'."

Mrs Merkel continued, "The Greeks finally saw sense and agreed that there was no alternative to seeing their economy obliterated, their assets confiscated, their population reduced to penury and starvation, and their sovereignty transferred to Berlin, along with the Parthenon.

"It is a win-win situation for us," said Mrs Merkel. "We win, and then we win again. We have got everything we wanted going into the deal, which was to save the euro and Europe's banks."

An exhausted Mr Tsipras said, "It's a great deal, although obviously not for Greece. But I can proudly tell my fellow countrymen that we haven't lost everything. At least we won the referendum and that's something we can tell our grandchildren about on Skype, when they have moved to Melbourne or Toronto."

Athens update

● There have been calls in Athens today for a fresh referendum to be held on the last referendum. The proposed ballot paper would offer the Greek electorate the choice of "Yes, that was a waste of time" or "No, there is no way that that wasn't a complete waste of time".

HOW A WEEK IN POLITICS HAS AGED GREEK LEADER

Monday July 6 **Monday July 13**

THE EYE'S MOST READ STORIES

Referendum 'to be an annual event'

As he confirmed plans for the Independence Referendum to run alongside the Edinburgh Festival as an annual event in Scotland, Alex Salmond brushed aside comments from David Cameron rejecting a second referendum.

"I heard David Cameron categorically say no to a second referendum, but everyone in the SNP knows when someone tells you 'no' it actually means 'yes'."

New television programme about cars to be made

A man who used to make television programmes about cars has confirmed he will now be making a new programme about cars for a different channel.

His two colleagues, who used to present the same programme about cars alongside the man, will also help to present the new show.

The new show will cover topics including a) cars, and b) more cars, which was also what people talked about on the old show.

On other pages

Is this the biggest broadcasting event of the century? No.

"How on earth did that get planning permission?"

𝌆𝌆𝌆𝌆 The Timons of Athens 𝌆𝌆𝌆𝌆

Friday 24 July 2015 BC

PROMETHEUS ACCEPTS PUNITIVE TERMS

BY OUR GREEK STAFF HARRY STOTTLE & HUGH CYDIDES

AT the eleventh hour, a tired Prometheus reluctantly accepted the terms of his deal with the father of the Gods, zEUs.

Under the new agreement, Prometheus will have his liver pecked out once a day for eternity.

"I thought I was just borrowing fire from the Gods," he said, "but they're treating me as if I've stolen it."

He continued, "This deal is not as bad as it looks, despite the eternal torment that is now guaranteed. The original offer on the table was to have my heart, lungs and testicles pecked out on an hourly basis. So in fact I think I've got off quite lightly."

Heracles and the twelve conditions

THE popular Greek hero Heracles was given an impossible task when yesterday he was handed a list of things he had to achieve by King EUrystEUs, in order to make up for his crimes of borrowing money from the Gods.

The labours are obviously designed to be impossible, but Heracles remained confident that he was capable of completing them all. The tasks he has been set include:

● Slay the many-headed Troika – you pay back one debt and immediately two more appear.

● Privatise the Golden Apples of the Hesperides.

● Obtain the girdle of Merkelyta, Queen of the Teutons.

● Capture the Luxembourgian Bore – (Jean-Claude Juncker).

● Deliver the Cretan Bull that everything's going to be fine.

● Clean out the unstable parliament's toilets after the latest budget cuts are announced.

We've got the idea. Ed.

I DON'T THINK MY BODY'S BEACH-READY YET

THOSE GOVERNMENT DEMANDS ON THE BBC

1. Stop making popular programmes which people like
2. Concentrate on unpopular programmes which people don't like
3. Then we can accuse you of being elitist and unpopular
4. And close you down!
5. Ha! Ha! Ha! Ha!
6. That'll teach you to be rude to us on Question Time

Open letter to PM shock

by Our Media Staff
Bea Beassey-Three

AN open letter to the Prime Minister from the friends of the *Daily Mail* was not received today.

Hundreds of the great and the good did not lend their names to an impassioned plea to save the *Daily Mail* from the threat of losing a few readers to the BBC website.

No one wrote about the consistent high quality of the *Daily Mail* over the past decades, and about the important role in public life that the *Mail* had provided, including supporting Hitler,

pointing out how badly Hugh Grant has aged compared to Colin Firth, and linking the increase of cancer to falling house prices.

Nor did anyone write to praise the unique creative minds behind the *Mail* online's "sidebar of shame", without which the general public would be utterly ill-informed about the wardrobe malfunctions of the cast of Towie, and how much weight obscure female celebrities are gaining or losing.

The letter doesn't conclude: "It would be a very sad day for Britain if the *Daily Mail* closed down forever."'

That 8-person independent Government board to review the future of the BBC

Rupert Murdoch Lord Rothermere Dirty Desmond The Barclay Brothers

Evgeny Lebedev's beard Simon Cowell The late Lord McAlpine Jeremy Clarkson

CLARE BALDING CLARE BALDING CLARE BALDING CLARE BALDING

"Have you been looking at Mail Online again?"

That BBC Celeb Letter You Won't Read

Dear Sir,

We the undersigned would like to make it clear that without the BBC none of us much-loved and famous people would have got where we are today (D Wing) and we would never have had the opportunity of reaching out and touching a younger audience, so don't let the government destroy the BBC – that's our job!

Of all the institutions of which we have been proud to be part, the BBC is still by far the best and most highly regarded – and the canteen is better than D Wing!

Yours the under-lock-and-key,
R. HARRIS,
S. HALL,
THE LATE J. SAVILE,
Etc etc...

(That's enough. Ed.)

POETRY CORNER

Lines on the departure of Mr James Naughtie from the BBC Today programme after 21 years

So. Farewell
Then "Jim" Naughtie.

Would you say that
You were best known
For asking your
Interviewees such
Long-winded and
Convoluted questions,
Intended, some people
Thought, to show how
Much you know about
The subject, that by
The end of your question
There was no time left
For your interviewee
To reply?

E.J. Thribb
(17½ minutes per question)

Nursery Times

FAMOUS LION CRUELLY KILLED BY WICKED HUNTER

By **Nicholas Witchell**

ALL of Narnia was in deepest mourning last night after the shocking news that its most loved and popular lion, Aslan, had been lured to his death by a ruthless and unscrupulous Minnesota dentist. (*Surely White Queen? Ed.*)

Conservationists rushed to express outrage at this dastardly action, led by Prince Charles *(surely Caspian? Ed.)*, who said, "It really is appalling that such an iconic creature should be slaughtered in this way.

"I'm going to write a letter to the White Queen making it clear that this kind of thing is totally unacceptable.

"Apart from anything else, this awful tragedy will be an absolute disaster for the Narnian tourist trade, just when more visitors were managing to get through the back of the wardrobe."

There has now been a huge backlash against the lion killer, which some people in Narnia feel has become disproportionate. Said one, "It's a witchhunt."

On other pages

● Did evil dentist kill Lion King? Walter Palmer accused of murdering musical star **2**
● Did dentist kill Bambi's mother? Walter Palmer accused of murdering fictional 1940's Disney character **3**
● Three bears complain that police won't come out to cottage after porridge burglary complaint **94**

Why wasn't the lion armed?

THE American National Rifle Association has intervened in the debate over Cecil the lion by pointing out that if only the lion had been armed, maybe things would have gone the other way.

"It's pretty plain to see what the problem here was", said a spokesman. "The lion had no gun. If it had just had a semi-automatic rifle, perhaps a shoulder-mounted cannon or even Colt and Wesson FleshTearer 3000, then maybe it would have had a chance at defending itself from the dentist in question. Sadly, the rules on carrying guns in Zimbabwe aren't as advanced as they are in the USA, meaning that the poor lion was defenceless in the face of this attack.

"Our new policy, Arm All Animals or AAA, would see creatures even as small as squirrels fitted with tiny guns they can use to defend themselves.

"The right to bear arms is not enough. We need to have the right to arm bears and indeed lions."

"Alright, that's enough!"

Daily Mail, Friday, August 21, 2015

MAIL 'DEFENDS BECKHAM PICTURES'

The Daily Mail has defended printing pictures of four-year-old Harper Beckham walking in the street with her dummy.

"He may be a dummy, but any picture of David Beckham still sells newspapers," said a spokesman yesterday.

"We printed the picture because we at the Mail are concerned that little Harper is ruining her teeth," said another spokeswoman.

"Mail Online is rightfully worried that little Harper's teeth mightn't develop properly and might end up all crooked and mangled. This means she won't be able to smile cheerfully when she's thirteen and we run a picture of her in a short skirt, saying how she's looking all grown up."

Zimbabwe outrage at manner of Cecil's death

Zimbabwe's President Robert Mugabe has joined the chorus of international condemnation about the manner in which US Dentist Walter Palmer killed Cecil the lion.

"Luring Cecil from his home, shooting him with a bow and arrow and then leaving him to suffer for forty hours before shooting him dead, that's being way too gentle."

"If Cecil the lion was one of the hundreds of political prisoners in my torture dungeons, he'd never have got off so lightly," the Zimbabwe dictator chuckled menacingly to reporters.

Andy Capp-in-Ring

HENRY DAVIES, TOM JAMIESON, NEV FOUNTAIN

YOU SEE JEREMY, YOU'LL NEVER BE LABOUR LEADER, BECAUSE OF ALL THAT HAMAS AND HEZBOLLAH NONSENSE...

YOU ASSOCIATE YOURSELF WITH NUTTERS, EXTREMISTS AND CRANKS...

AND I'VE NEVER DONE THAT.

ED MILIBAND DOESN'T COUNT!

OBAMA'S TRIUMPHANT VISIT TO AFRICA

by Our Africa Staff **Ken Yah**

AS Air Force One touched down at Nairobi's newly renamed Barack Obama airport, Kenya's most famous son President Obama was greeted by two million jubilant Kenyans in full tribal costume of suits and ties.

The president stepped onto the tarmac and received an ecstatic ovation when his opening words were "Ich bin ein Afrikaaner".

He was welcomed by Kenya's hereditary president, Uhuru Kenyatta, son of the country's founding dictator, Omo Kenyatta, known for his 1963 election slogan, "Omo washes whites out".

Out of Africa into Europe

The president went out of his way to praise what he described as "the continent of the future".

"Wherever I go in this great continent of ours," he said, having only just arrived, "I am amazed by what can only be described as the astonishing renaissance in Africa's economic fortunes."

To the huge pleasure of his vast audience, he then climaxed his speech with a carefully prepared soundbite which was designed to make headlines from Cape to Cairo, from Eritrea to the Yemen, from Libya to the Congolese Democratic Dictatorship.

"Africa," he proclaimed, "is on the move." At these words, several million Africans proved his point by boarding small, leaking vessels heading for a new life in camps outside Calais (via Lampedusa, Lesbos, Malta, Sicily, France etc).

To those who were left, the president said, "If my folks could get out of Africa in search of a better life, I'm sure you guys can do the same. God bless Africa."

Cameron orders Britons to leave UK

by Our Travel Staff **E.C. Jet**

Prime Minister David Cameron last night told the Foreign Office to instruct all British citizens to leave the country at once because it is "no longer safe".

After raising the threat level of terrorism from "highly likely" to a "no brainer", the FCO advised Britons to go abroad to countries which are "very much safer".

Isis? What Isis?

Following this shock announcement, millions of Britons protested that they had no wish to leave the country where they had been enjoying weeks of sunshine, an exceptional Wimbledon and a rare victory over Australia in the test match.

"We feel totally safe here in Britain," said a London couple, Cyd and Boris Johnson, as they sat in deckchairs under a cloudless sky. "Wherever we go, we see policemen carrying guns, so we don't know what Mr Cameron is on about.

"To make us leave London would be just giving in to the terrorists."

The Foreign Office is now suggesting that British citizens should seek political asylum in Tunisia, where security has recently been stepped up to such a level that "no one is ever likely to be a victim of terrorism again".

"Don't worry about them, Mr Migrant, I've been warning them since Paris what would happen if they didn't stop squabbling"

IRAN NUCLEAR DEAL – SANCTIONS OVER

Great, can we now buy some plutonium?

"He's beach-body ready!"

IT'S THE HIT NEW GAME FROM THE US

Can you win the nomination for the Republican candidacy? Hours of fun!

Donald

Ridiculousness of hair	94
Lame environmental views	94
Neanderthal-style sexism	94
Gross racial stereotyping	94
Overall general stupidity	100

POETRY CORNER

**In Memoriam
Omar Sharif, legendary screen actor**

So. Farewell
Then Omar Sharif,
Star of Lawrence of
Arabia and Dr Zhivago and
Lots of other films.

You were in Funny Girl
With Barbra Streisand
And in Barbra Streisand
During Funny Girl.

You were in Mayerling
With Catherine Deneuve
And in Catherine Deneuve
During Mayerling.

You were in The Burglars
With Dyan Cannon
And in...

Yes alright! We get
The idea. Ed.

> E.J. Heart Thribb
> (Certificate 17½)

**In Memoriam
Omar Sharif,
international bridge player**

So. Farewell
Then Omar Sharif.

You were dealt
A good hand,
Made some great
Contracts and broke
Many hearts.

But now the last
Trump has sounded
And we must bid you
Farewell.

> E.J. Thribb (17½ Spades)

DIARY

MARINA WARNER: WHAT IS A STORY?

What is a story? The dictionary definition is "a book that lists the words of a language in alphabetical order and gives their meaning". But this is, it should be added, less a dictionary definition per se, than the definition of a dictionary. Yes, it goes a certain way towards an understanding of story, but perhaps not far enough.

As the great Afro-Caribbean poet, Ab-Sol Ut-Borr, who was raised by Bedouin parents in Mozambique, from where he moved early in life to Haslemere, before transporting his home and family across the border to Fernhurst, famously said: "A story is never just a story but a story about a story". Or, in other words, the story of a story is a story of the story within the story. Or, viewed from another perspective, the story within a story is not just the story of the story but the story of the story within the story of the story."

Wise words, indeed.

But what exactly is a story? By revealing our past, the writer helps us define our future; by defining our future, the writer helps reveal our past. The author of novels is both light and dark, up and down, cross and blackwell, little and large, pinky and perky, over and out. Fiction is, for many, an optimistic form, but for others it bestrides our universe with an angry pessimism. A story is, perhaps above all else, a tale. But what exactly do we mean when we talk of a tale? According to my dictionary, a tale is "the hindmost part of an animal, especially when extended beyond the rest of the body, such as the flexible extension of the backbone or the feathers at the hind end of a bird." But, to many contemporary authors, it is both more and less than that. As world famous novelist and internationally respected literary critic Eve E. Gowing so memorably puts it: "It is the duty of the artist to examine us, to diagnose our condition, and then – and only then – to suggest a cure". But in the event of anything more serious, do please consult your local GP.

As the Chairman of the International Man Booker Prize, I was incessantly struck over the head – again and again and again and, so to speak, again – by the sheer weight of sensitive works of fiction arriving kicking and screaming through my letter box day after day, or, to put it another way, on a daily basis.

Each one of them raised a vast landscape of unanswered questions in my mind, questions like Who? What? Where? When? and, perhaps above all, Why?

Is an author responsible for telling the truth even if the truth he or she tells is, by its very nature, made up? Can the same author be too made up, or is there always a crying need for a really solid foundation? Who am I? and, more importantly, Who are you and what on earth are you doing here? Does an author have an obligation to be authentic? And is there perhaps a difference between authenticity and orthodontistry?

The short story writer Miguel-Antonio Salvador Ramirez-Lopez – who, when last measured by the committee of the International Man Booker Prize, which I chaired, came up to just 4ft 9ins in his socks – is, like so many people, a Mexican born in South Wales whose grandparents became part of the great Mexican-Welsh diaspora, ending up in the Finnish quarter of Guadeloupe, from where he writes his beautifully-honed stories in his unique blend of Catalan and Urdu. Significantly, his intensely symphonic stories, many of them well under two or three words long, but charged with his own deeply-held fusion of illusion, elusion, elision, attrition and emission, serve to remind us of how intensely short a short story can be.

Potent, mysterious, unpredictable and insinuating: these are four, arguably five, words that, on several levels, continue to maintain an essentially verbal existence. It was, I think, the unjustly neglected Peruvian novelist Nurofen Cortizone de Benitez Espinoza, the creator of Manuel de la Plaza, one of the most memorable cockatoos in recent Peruvian fiction, who famously said, "The story is a diving board, the reader is the pool, and the writer is the swimming costume" though, later in life, he was to profoundly upset academics and students alike by changing his mind and making the reader the swimming costume, the writer the diving board, and the story the pool.

Tomorrow, I shall again be asking the question, "What is a story?", only this time in reverse: "Story a is what?"

As told to
CRAIG BROWN

"Have you tried St John's Wort?"

HARPER LEE THIRD BOOK DISCOVERED

After the literary event of the year, with the release of the long-awaited sequel to *To Kill A Mocking Bird*, the publishing world is buzzing with rumours that a possible third manuscript takes the story even further.

According to insiders, in the new book, the lawyer hero Atticus Finch, aged 95, posts pictures of himself on Facebook with a Confederate flag, before going crazy with a handgun in an old people's home where Scout is now working. One critic said, "This may disappoint liberals even more than the last one".

JEFFREY ARCHER NEW BOOK LOST

There was relief today as Jeffrey Archer's editor said he had no idea where the manuscript of Jeffrey Archer's new novel had gone. "He delivered it to me and I'm afraid it must have disappeared. Now nobody will ever read it. What a shame."

It was quite obvious that he was lying, the editor not Jeffrey, but no one queried it. However, there are fears that Jeffrey Archer will write another one this evening, possibly called *To Mock a Killing Bird*, which he will later claim is an entirely original idea about an epic miscarriage of justice, involving a brave author whose useless lawyer failed to stop him going to prison for perjury.

McLACHLAN

Your Guide to Finches

GREENFINCH   HAWFINCH   GOLDFINCH   BULLFINCH

CHAFFINCH   ATTICUSFINCH

CALAIS IN PICTURES

FRENCH POLICE PASSIVE

We categorically deny we're turning our back on the problem

FRENCH POLICE ACTIVE

You're not supposed to be here...

Go to Britain!

THE MIGRANT EUROTUNNEL CRISIS
HOW IT WORKS

DAY 5 Government orders increased Eurotunnel security to stop desperate immigrants.

DAY 6 Thousands of desperate immigrants at Calais storm the tunnel and look for work.

DAY 9 Desperate immigrants discover the only people hiring unskilled foreigners are G4S.

DAY 15 Desperate immigrants employed by G4S security as guards to police the tunnel to stop any more desperate immigrants getting into Britain.

DAY 21 Economy surges

FINANCIAL TIMES
Friday 7 August 2015

Top British brand sold to Japan

by Our Business Staff **Nikkei Robinson**

For years two letters have been synonymous with the very best of Britain. Those two simple letters have summed up everything that a bona fide British bluechip institution aspires to be – a byword for independence, quality and class.

But now, Japan has bought the UK. And questions must be asked as to how we have let the ultimate symbol of Britain pass into Far Eastern hands.

Surely the UK was worth keeping, even if it has had problems in the recent past and critics are claiming it is not as good as it was?

Known to generations as the "pink 'un", named after the colour of its global empire on the world map, the UK now faces an uncertain future as it struggles to retain its identity as part of a giant Eastern conglomerate.

Said one former UK fan, "You used to be able to rely on the UK, but now – who knows? It will probably be turned into a theme park."

Late news
Financial Times to be renamed "The Rising Sun".

Case Study from the DWP

Iain, aged 53, is one of the legal success stories of our "Get the Disabled Into Work Programme".

Five years ago, Iain was considered wholly unemployable. He had once briefly held down a job as Leader of the Tory Party, but was soon sacked on the grounds that he was "sadly unfit for purpose".

But now under this government scheme, Iain is a new man. Every day he can go proudly into an office, where he is treated with respect by his colleagues; and under our new "More Than Living Wage" scheme, he is able to take home £134,000 a year.

Says Iain, "I've been very lucky to have been so generously helped by this government. Without these new schemes, I might well have had to spend the rest of my life unemployed and living on benefits, costing the taxpayer a fortune.

"As it is, I have been allowed back into the world of work, which has done wonders for my self-respect and it means I'm not sitting around all day in my father-in-law's house getting under the feet of my dear wife and chief carer Betsy."

WARNING This Real Life Story is not actually true. It has been compiled by the DWP from a number of similar stories in order to help the public to understand better how marvellous David Cameron's Conservative Party really is.

BEWARE OF SEAGULLS

"He's beak-body ready..."

SPOT THE DIFFERENCE

Old peer in bra

Sewell

New peer in bra

Mone

Shame of old man in prostitute and cocaine scandal

by Our Sun Staff
N. Trapment

An elderly grandee faced disgrace today when it was revealed that he had taken part in organising a debauched sex party story.

Mr Rupert Murdoch, the proprietor of the Sun newspaper, was facing public humiliation for his sleazy role in the tawdry Lord Sewel affair.

Mr Murdoch was caught red-handed owning the sex-mad newspaper which quite clearly set up Lord Sewel with the hookers and arranged the filming of the Labour peer as he takes cocaine and answers questions on the relative merits of the Labour leadership candidates.

Porn Baron

Said one observer, "Murdoch really should be ashamed of himself. At his age he should be playing with his grandchildren. Instead, he is up to his neck in filth."

He continued, "It's his kids I feel sorry for. Oh, no I don't. They're as bad as he is."

Rupert Murdoch is 94.

KNOW YOUR MEN:

ALPHA MALE   ALFALFA MALE

THE CILLA WHO KNEW ME

by **Everyone**

THERE are few people the nation takes to their hearts with such passion that they refer to them by a single name: Me.

Cilla was lucky enough to have met me way back in the 1960s, and right through my varied and interesting career, Cilla was always there, somewhere.

The Beatles, Burt Bacharach, the Royal Family, they all met me and I introduced them to Cilla.

From the Cavern to the London Palladium to the Royal Variety Show, mine was a dazzling trajectory – but through it all I kept the common touch – and Cilla always said to me, "Fame hasn't changed you, chuck, you're still the famous, brilliant star you always were."

The last time Cilla saw me was just a month ago and I was looking tanned and healthy and was living life to the full.

Who are we talking about again? Oh, yes. Me.

© *All newspapers.*

FUNNIEST JOKE IN EDINBURGH

by Our Fringe Staff **Hans Free** and **Nick Jokes**

This year's award for the funniest joke on the Fringe goes, yet again, to Alex Salmond. The joke "the BBC is Britain's Pravda" came in the middle of his hilarious extended monologue on the inadequacies of the BBC, and earned him the title Scotland's Ex-First Minister of Mirth.

THOSE ALEX SALMOND ZINGERS:

"My dog has no nose… yet nowhere did this fact appear in any of Nick Robinson's biased and wholly inaccurate reports"

"My wife's gone to the West Indies… there she'll try and recuperate from the stresses of enduring the daily misrepresenting of SNP policy made by the Tory lapdog Robinson"

"What's Brown and v Sticky?… That would of course be Nick Robinson spouting the same old tired old Labour propaganda which discredits him and brings ignominy on the wretched Biased Broadcasting Corporation"

Facebook 'Billion Day' milestone

by Our Technology Reporter
Samantha Click

There was widespread joy throughout Silicon Valley after Facebook founder Mark Zuckerberg revealed that he'd made a billion pounds in a single day for a first time.

"Facebook has always been about more than just pious platitudes bringing people around the world together, it's been about irritating pop-up ads and clickbait autoplay video making me shedloads of money on which I don't pay any tax," Zuckerberg posted on the site.

"But there will be no resting on our laurels. Facebook will continue to develop ever more innovative ways to trick you into viewing ads so as to further enrich the experience of being me."

Zuckerberg's "billion day" announcement on Facebook itself broke records for the most number of likes a single post has received from his bank manager.

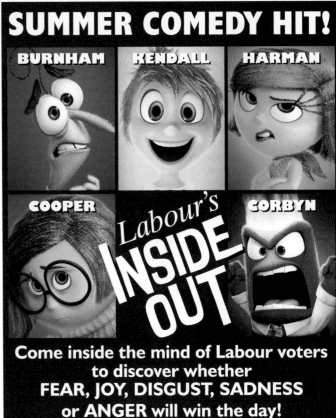

DIARY
KANYE WEST: BLOWN MA OWN NOSE

See the thing is, as I was sayin', I got me a sniffle, don' do much skiffle, and what I'm sayin' is, I'm here to relinquish and extinguish that distinguish' sniff, man, let's riff, you know what I'm sayin'?

For me as Kanye West, I got to fuck shit up, nose-wise. I'm here to crack the pavement with my nose-blown', to break new ground in the whole blowin'-nose, blow-nosin' arena, I'm seein' ya, 'cos it's a blow-nose scenario, like Super Mario, too heavy to carry-o, this is the music of the mucus, so we not gonna let it spook us.

Blow, man, blow. Blow like you could die tomorrow. Go for it. But first thing, you bring out your handkerchief, 'cos there's no nose worth blowin' that ain't worth blowin' on a handkerchief. And no handkerchief ain't good 'nuff for Kanye West's nose that ain't been designed, refined, signed and inclined, wined and dined, by the man hisself, Kanye West, in his special Blow Your Nose for Justice $5,000 edition for Louis Vuitton, so let's fuck this shit up, man, let's blow, man, blow, let's sound the end to no more nasal negativity, but let's do it in style, like Picasso or Matisse, cos that's the way that is, or Van Gogh, jeez, see that man go.

That's how life is. Is a nose-blow. You could just be livin' your own life, hangin' out, bangin' out, wangin' out, lookin' for motivation in your recreation, then from outta nowhere it happens, it just happens, you get this sniff, turns to a riff, an' all at once your sniff is a sniffle, erect as a nipple, like a ripple on sea, between you and me, and so you think it'll go but it won't go, it's slow to depart, don't know when to depart, so you say Jeez, you know the only way out, please, is to sneeze, no win, no fees.

I do product, design clothes, design architecture, design works of genius, design for the future like there's no tomorrow, everything you could think about, so when I wanna go blow my nose, the first thing I say is, "Hey, wait a second – there's no handkerchief in the world today that

PRINCE GEORGE IN NEW ROW

Stop invading my privacy!

is beautiful and dutiful and fruitiful 'nuff to be blowin' the nose of Kanye West – and there's only one dude can design the best, that's this guy West that looks like me and sounds like me and you know why? Cos he is me, and now he's settin' himself the task, the big ask, the water in the flask, the man behind the mask, like the baskin' shark who carries the flask, and that task, since you ask, is designin' the square of material, let's get weary y'all, and I'll make it not too slim too wide too short or too lanky, 'cos – you now what I'm sayin'? – this is my hankie.

So now you know, you got yo' nose to blow, an' you already been designin' yosel' the world's greatest handkerchief known to man, that's gonna add to the whole of humanity, let's not talk inanity, what we want is sanity, hey, you seen that manatee tha's in the zoo, so whatcha gonna do, man, you know whatchado, you get ready to blow, go, go, go, nice and deep and low, that's how you sho' do it when you gotta blow it, you don't stow it, you throw it, right out into the air, who cares if people stare. But where is my hankie now I need it, don't recede it, it's not a book, take a look, you cannot read it, but you must heed it, indeed it's a creed, it's a kind of a tissue for when you go atishoo, but that's now what's at issue, not when you're married to Kim Kardashian, and yo' plannin' go "atishoo" an', you'll be brought to yo knees by one huge massive sneeze, yeah, you gotta avoid it, this boy he done good in the 'hood when he could, but he never wore no long V necks, not when reachin' for his Extra-Strong Kleenex.

Like, when I compare myself to Steve Jobs, Dr Martin Luther King, Walt Disney, Maya Angelou, Michael Jackson or whoever, it's because I'm tryin' to show the world a little bit of context to the possibilities that are in front of me, so like today I'm at breakfast with Anna Wintour an' at lunch with Jay Z and at cocktails with Karl Lagerfeld, an' that makes me like Shakespeare or Tolstoy or whoever, I've got all these thoughts and innovations I want to pursue, I so creative, I create like a child, I wake up one morning and say, "I feel like a sneeze, but no kerchief is up to the job, so I'm gonna design me a kerchief, so I get to phone Balmain and Diesel and Fendi, "I just drew me a kerchief, nine inches by nine inches, it's like a perfect square and all white, whiter than white, clean outtasight, this kerchief gonna blow you away". An' they all wanna market my handkerchief because they know like I know and you know and the world know that the handkerchief designed by Kanye West is the best and most expensive handkerchief in the whole wide world, you got twenty million people screaming for it, so don't tell me I don't deserve to design a handkerchief, jeez, I'm the Picasso of the handkerchief.

So now what we got, we got Kanye West Premiere Deluxe Rappin' Handkerchief sellin' for $1,500, and for the superior nose we got the Kanye West Supa-Special Bring Justice to the World VVVIP Deluxe Rappin' Handkerchief sellin' for $250,000, with diamonds and all that shit sewn into the sides, is genius, 'cos as a creative artist you gotta take risks, you gotta take the modderfockin risks, without the sneeze there's ain't no blow, know what I'm saying?

As told to
CRAIG BROWN

Out-Of-Date Proverbs

'There's Plenty More Fish in the Sea'

'A Trouble Shared is a Trouble Halved'

'Neither a Borrower Nor a Lender Be'

'Fear Greeks Bearing Gifts'

'There's Safety in Numbers'

WHY JEREMY CORBYN IS WINNING THE LABOUR LEADERSHIP — IN FULL

I'm not Jeremy Corbyn, I'm just an old bloke!

NICHOLAS

Alastair Campbell's stark warning, 'We're less than 45 days away from disaster'

by Our Political Staff
W.M. Deedes

THE former Labour spin doctor Alastair Campbell last night told the party that it was on the brink of destruction and that if it did not take firm action at once, it would be obliterated.

Campbell said that he had compiled a secret dossier, taken from the internet, largely Mail online, which proved conclusively that if Jeremy Corbyn was not removed from power then Britain would be under attack from a man he called "a crazed dictator who wants to destroy everything in the United Kingdom".

Critics immediately claimed that Campbell had "sexed up" his report and that there was actually no evidence that Jeremy Corbyn was "a weapon of Mass Destruction".

Campbell, however, stood by his dodgy dossier and swore by his original story.

"It's fucking true," he said. "What we have here is a clearly demented, crazed ideologue who will stop at nothing to get his way. But enough of me."

He concluded, "The Labour Party is at war and what it needs is a really good Peace Envoy like my old friend Tony Blair."

Jeremy Corbyn is 94.

That Tony Blair Labour leadership speech in full

"I'm not annoying you, am I?"

"Me...me...me...me...me...me... me...me...me...me..."*(Cont. for all eternity)*

WORLD ATHLETICS CHAMPIONSHIPS

Those events in full...

- 100mg injection
- 200mg injection
- Legal Hurdles
- High Jump
- Legal High Jump
- Triple Dose
- Shot-of-EPO-put
- 10,000mg injection
  (That's enough drugs. Ed)

New Strictly Line-Up
Who will be in the BBC's new Spanglorama? You decide...

Camila Batmanghelidjh

Julian Assange

Harper Beckham

Sir John Chilcot

Mel 'n' Sue

Len McCluskey

The late Queen Nefertiti

Anjem Choudary

Quick! Quick! Slow! Quick! Call now while BBC lasts

Neasden Central Police Station

0830 hrs Inspector Uxbridge goes on the prestigious "Good Morning, Neasden" breakfast TV show to make the following very important statement:

"The Neasden Police Service is very proud to announce that we have now become the 94th force in the country to be pursuing an active and top-priority investigation into the paedophile activities of the late Sir Edward Heath.

This gentleman was very famous and appeared frequently on national television in the 1970s. This alone aroused our suspicions that Heath could well have been involved in paedophilic offences of the type with which we have become familiar from the similar record of the late Sir James Savile, both of whom significantly appeared together in this incriminating and deeply shocking photograph.

If you feel that you recognise either of these men and that they might have subjected you to historic sexual abuse at any time between the years 1937 and 2005, the Neasden police station is now operating a 24-hour special helpline which you can contact to arrange an interview with specially trained officers from our new 50-strong unit, known as Operation Yewtube."

0852 hrs All officers summoned to central briefing room to hear inspirational address from Inspector Uxbridge, announcing that Neasden police force would no longer have the time or resources to investigate minor crimes, such as burglary. In future, officers would only attend call-outs to burglaries when these had occurred in properties with even numbers.

0936 hrs Desk Sergeant Hainault reported receipt of calls from the public asking for assistance following burglaries at various addresses, including 13, 49, 63 and 121 Poundstretcher Lane, and 23 and 79 Pricerite Crescent. In compliance with new station policy, the sergeant correctly ignored all these calls and continued with his researches into old video film showing the late Mr Heath in a suspicious white jacket, conducting an orchestra, waving his hands about in an "unnatural manner".

1105 hrs Desk Sergeant Hainault receives new series of calls reporting burglarious activity at a number of properties in Lidl Road, viz numbers 2, 4, 6, 8 and 10. The desk sergeant consults his line manager, Detective Inspector Barnet, who informs him of new station policy not to attend call-outs to properties with even numbers either, on grounds that all officers are now required to prioritise watching old videos of Mr Heath surrounded by suspicious-looking foreign persons as he signs a piece of paper at undisclosed location in Europe.

1230 hrs Lunch in Slug & Pleb.

Even I feel sorry for my old enemy Ted Heath

by Lord Normo of Tebbs

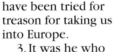

NO ONE could accuse me of apologising for that cold fish, the late Sir Edward Heath; an aloof and arrogant man for whom I had nothing but contempt throughout his dismal and treacherous political career.

Indeed, there are a great many things you could say about Ted Heath, but being a paedophile was never one of them.

The things you could say, however, are the following:

1. He was the worst prime minister we've ever had.

2. It was he who should have been tried for treason for taking us into Europe.

3. It was he who brought Britain to its knees with the 3-day week.

4. And worst of all, it was he who constantly tried to undermine the best prime minister the world has ever seen, my old friend Margaret Thatcher.

Surely all this is enough to damn Mr Heath for ever as an utterly worthless and disgraced public figure, without us having to make up a lot of silly rubbish about him being a *(cont. p94)*

Shock as breasts found on internet

THERE was outrage today as internet browsers suddenly stumbled across a pair of breasts performing their natural function.

Said one appalled web user, "I don't go surfing when my wife's asleep to be confronted with this kind of sight.

"Everyone knows breasts should only be seen beneath the face of a pouting porn star, or dangling alluringly over a naked man, or woman – I'm not fussy. Now, if you'll excuse me, I'm late for the House of Lords."

Mastermind meets Dad's Army

"And your name is…?"   *"Don't tell him, Pike"*

Daily Mailograph

Friday 21 August 2015

10 Reasons Why Voting For Corbyn Will Lead to Civil War

1. Corbyn once had a cat called Harold Wilson, the man who MI5 rightly accused of being a Soviet spy.
2. Corbyn's initials are JC, a deliberate and offensive attempt to present himself as the Messiah.
3. Corbyn has met many of the world's most unpleasant dictators and never once sold them any arms.
4. Corbyn claims the smallest amount of expenses as an MP, disloyally making his fellow MPs look bad and bringing the whole system into disrepute.
5. Corbyn has been married at least three times – and divorced at least twice.
6. Corbyn's current wife sells Fairtrade coffee instead of upmarket stationery like proper party leaders' wives.
7. His brother is called Piers, who is a weather forecaster, proving that "getting everything wrong" runs in the family.
8. Corbyn has a beard. If he can't be bothered to shave, can he bothered to run the country?
9. Corbyn wears hats and you know what my mother says about men who wear hats.
10. Corbyn was a known associate of Tony Benn who, according to the obituary in this newspaper, was a "much-loved national treasure, whose integrity and commitment were admired on all sides of the political divide". *(You're fired. Ed)*

IRA defends current activities

by Our Northern Ireland Correspondent **Dave Javoogh**

As evidence emerged that the IRA might once more engaged in revenge killings and punishment beatings, the organisation made this statement, delivered yesterday by a spokesman wearing a freshly-knitted balaclava.

"We are simply returning to our core values from the '70s and '80s," he announced, speaking through a wool/polyester/cotton mix.

"These are values that we had sadly lost when our party got taken over by professional politicians who were more interested in getting into power rather than enacting the traditional principles of violence upon which our party was founded.

"Perhaps now we can offer a proper alternative to peaceful democracy that our rank and file members have been crying out for."

CAMERON ON HOLIDAY AS IMMIGRATION HITS RECORD HIGH

Nothing seems to work

Including you!

Our borders are useless

Speak for yourself!

PM criticised for huge numbers 'swarming in'

by Our Immigration Staff
Peter Seaborne

David Cameron was under growing pressure last night over his failure to keep his promise of cutting the number of those entering the UK's House of Lords to "less than 100,000".

Lordswatch, the pressure group which monitors the number of migrants gaining access to the upper chamber, said there were "at least 300,000 new members of the Lords this week alone".

The Prime Minister, however, defended his actions, claiming that the vast majority of the new Lords were bona fide refugees from his own government and desperately needed somewhere to sit down and be paid a living wage.

THOSE DISILLUSION HONOURS IN FULL

Lord Hedge of Fund, formerly Johnny Hedgefund, CEO of leading investment group Bastard Asset Management.

Lord Donor of Kebab, formerly Efti Donor, chairman of leading charity Fast Food For Tories.

Lord Bogus of Claim, formerly Alec Douglas-Second-Home, junior MP who commendably handed back £237,000 in expenses after he mistakenly claimed for sending all his children to Eton.

Lord Dead of Beat, formerly Simon Timeserver, Cabinet Minister under the last three Conservative Administrations.

Lord Server of Time, formerly Roger Deadbeat, Cabinet Minister under the last one Liberal Administration.

Lord Batman of Robbin, formerly Robin Batmanjellyandcustard, prominent supporter of top charity You-Must-Be-Kidding Company.

David Mellors, BEM, under-gardener to the Prime Minister for services to trimming wisteria (£680 cash-in-hand, thanks guv)

Rock Cakes, CBE, body-board surfing coach to the Prime Minister and family. Sole proprieter of Polzeath's Tory Wetsuit Rentals.

Vidal L'Oreal, OBE, hairdresser to the Prime Minister. Because he's worth it.

GOVERNMENT PLAN TO BOMB SYRIA

From The Message Boards

Members of the online community respond to the major issues of the day...

Pensioner seeks naked cleaner

I was disgusted to hear of the old man in Bristol who advertised for a female ("20-55, any shape") to clean in the nude while he watches, for the princely sum of £20 an hour. This follows similar arrangements with previous women, who "shared a glass of wine" with him afterwards (though you'd have thought he could have pushed the boat out and given them their own glass). He says he remains friends with them, that his antics are "not illegal" and that there is "nothing sexual" about it. So why my disgust at this amicable arrangement? Because the asexual consensual gawper brazenly describes himself as "a voyeur"! In a desperate attempt to talk up his dreary suburban hobby, this sad man tries to align himself with that daring band of brothers who perch in precarious "hides", illicitly install hidden cameras, and risk their liberty to covertly enjoy womankind in her most thrilling state: bare and unaware. – *Monkey see*

you voyer's must be the only peple hopin to raise UNAWARENESS for your cause! lolz – *Danny Daz*

make's sense the cleaner cant pinch his valuable's, noware to hide them ☺ – *Hunny pot*

she should charge extra for pinching his valuable's! lolz – *Danny Daz*

Why no complaints about discrimination against men over 55? – *I pay but have no say*

There are strong health and safety grounds for not employing elderly males in this role. The medical literature shows that this demographic is disproportionately likely to sustain penile injuries caused by vacuum cleaners, most of which occur while "cleaning in nude", often in situations where the machine "switched itself on" and attacked the hapless victim. – *Dr Finlay's Bookcase*

When working as a male office cleaner, I fell victim to a devious voyeuristic honey trap. As a sitophiliac with a high sex drive, I was tempted by a sumptuous bowl of fruit left as bait, and couldn't resist the coquettish charms of one particularly pert peach. (They really shouldn't flaunt their furry little bottoms like that!) CCTV and prurient security guards sealed my fate. – *Five a day*

I refuse to demean women by employing cleaners on the minimum wage, so at considerable expense I hire ladies from a role-playing escort agency instead. French Maid outfits are practical and healthy, with the short skirt and stockings providing plenty of ventilation. There is no question of any impropriety. – *Maurice*

not bein funny but y not get a normle cleaner with normle clothe's and pay her more? – *Hayley 321*

It's a point of principle. You wouldn't understand. – *Maurice*

Nursery Times

Friday, Once-upon-a-time

KIDS' CHARITY TO CLOSE?

By Our Investigative Team **Richard North-Pole & John Snowflake**

THE larger-than-life children's charity founder, Santa Claus, was under investigation last night after allegations of financial impropriety.

For years, the colourfully dressed, roly-poly do-gooder has been handing out presents to all the children of the world, but now accountants are questioning how such largesse could possibly be funded. There are also questions about whether children received gifts irrespective of whether they were "naughty or nice".

Said one insider, "I saw children go into Santa's grotto and come out with iPods. One boy came out with a spliff. It was like Christmas Day every day round at Santa's."

Also involved in the investigation is one of Santa's little helpers, the bearded elf known as "Botney", who was meant to oversee the affairs of Santa's philanthropic enterprise, but who failed to stop Santa flying all over the world in a first-class sleigh and charging it all on expenses.

Others embroiled in the collapse of the charity include top supporter David the Red-Faced Cameron, who saw Santa as a charismatic figure who would make him look good by taking over the state's responsibility for giving children hand-outs. *(Is this right? Ed.)*

DING! DONG! THE WITCH ISN'T DEAD!

THE Wicked Witch of the West, who everyone thought had melted under pressure in the Nurseryland Court, has made a dramatic return to run the Emerald News Corps.

Said the Wizened of Oz, "Strewth, mate – the wicked witch was completely cleared of being wicked and I'm delighted to welcome her back to carry on wielding her broom and getting her team of flying monkeys to harass all the munchkins." The cowardly lion commented, "The Wizened of Oz must be scared of her, I know I am." While his colleague, the scarecrow, added, "He's clearly lost his brain!"

HOW GOVERNMENT POLICY WORKS Pt. 94

Elderly homecare funding today

Elderly homecare funding tomorrow

"We're collecting for older people whose lives have been ruined by charities collecting from older people"

93

What Next For The Chinese Dragon?

by Our Economics Expert
Hu Nohz

AS the Chinese economy slows inexorably, spreading uncertainty across the globe, serious questions are now being asked.

Has the fabled Chinese dragon finally run out of puff? Is the fire going out? Will the dragon ever soar into the air again? Have its golden scales lost their sheen? Is it retreating into its cave? And is the dragon's hoard of treasure nothing more than a legend? Are its teeth blunted? And its wings clipped? And has it run out of puff? Is the fire going out? *(continued pages 2-94 of all papers)*

GREAT FALL OF CHINA

That Takeaway Menu in Full

Black Monday Bean Sauce

– ✳ –

Peking Duck-up

– ✳ –

Dim Bankers Sum

– ✳ –

Sweet & Sour Taste in the Mouth

– ✳ –

Someone-for-the-Chop Suey

– ✳ –

Stir-Crazy Noodles

– ✳ –

Prawn Total Crackers

– ✳ –

Lost-a-Fortune Cookie

To Drink: *Rice Whine*

WARNING: Prices may go down as well as up

Time for action

PICTURE that changed the world... heartbreaking scenes across Europe... desperate tide of humanity... worst refugee crisis since World War Two... only those with hearts of stone could not agree that something must be done... Mrs Merkel's magnanimous gesture shows the way... we must open our hearts and borders... Mr Cameron quite right to follow suit... offering sanctuary to 20,000 Syrians is the least we can do... of course practical realities must not be forgotten... housing, hospitals, school places... is 20,000 too many... no time for knee-jerk reactions... easy to become swept away on a tide of emotion... giving a home to even 20,000 will not make the slightest difference to the overall refugee crisis... root problem lies in Syria... must not repeat mistakes of Iraq and Libya... vital not to take precipitate action... indeed, best policy would be to recognise that this is a time for no action.

© *All newspapers.*

SPOT THE DIFFERENCE

All Newspapers: August 2015

SWARM OF ILLEGAL MIGRANTS EN ROUTE TO BRITAIN

All Newspapers: September 2015

HEROIC REFUGEES MAKE PERILOUS JOURNEY ACROSS EUROPE IN SEARCH OF A BETTER LIFE

GERMANY TURNS BACK REFUGEES

We are only obeying borders

Sarah Vain

It's all about me!

SO Barrister Charlotte Proudman has got a male admirer.

Who hasn't?! I get men writing to me all the time, asking if they can have a picture of me in my scanties, but you don't find me rushing into print about it.

No, I don't go on and on about the legions of blokes, panting over the picture of me (see above).

If a man can't compliment a beautiful woman (like me, which they do often BTW) then what's the world coming to?

So come on you ghastly Feminazi, have a sense of humour, like me, and roll with the punches, like I do. You've had more than your fair share of column inches, now let's talk about something more important, namely – ME!

Dave Snooty AND HIS PEDIGREE CHUMS

THE FIRST 100 DAYS OF THE CORBYN PREMIERSHIP

THIS nightmare vision of Britain's immediate future, as it is taken over by a mad Trotskyite dictator, will shock you to the core – unless you've already read it in all the other papers.

What, however, is really shocking is that this dystopian vision is not some idle fantasy. *EVERY WORD OF IT IS TRUE.*

Day One

Prime Minister Corbyn refuses to meet the Queen and calls for her abdication.

Day Two

Corbyn, now to be known as Comrade Prime Minister, appoints his new Cabinet. Top posts will go to Gerry Adams as Secretary of State for Defence, Anjem Choudary as Home Secretary, Camila Batmanjellybean as Chancellor of the Exchequer and Russell Brand as Secretary of State in Charge of Benefits for Work and Pensions.

Day Three

Corbyn nationalises all industries without compensation and orders the City of London to be closed down and reopened as a Museum of Capitalism.

Twenty thousand banks are to be put on trial for crimes against The People, under new Justice Minister, ex-Guardian columnist Owen Jones.

Day Four

The FTSE collapses to zero, and sterling drops to its lowest ever level of parity with the Zimbabwean dollar and North Korean kim.

Day Five

The great helmsman Corbyn signs treaty with Putin, allowing all Britain's nuclear missiles to be transferred to Russia, while Trident submarines are to be given as a goodwill gesture to the People's Navy of China.

Day Six

New US President Hillary Clinton protests to Britain about its nuclear deal with Russia and the armed seizing of all US assets in the UK, as reparation for America's support of Israeli war crimes. Corbyn's response, after Cobra meeting with his new Chief of the Defence Staff George Galloway, and Head of Intelligence Julian Assange, is to declare war on the US.

Day Seven

China and Russia support Britain, and World War Three begins.

Meanwhile, Corbyn, now known as the "Supreme Leader", orders the execution of all "bourgeois, revisionist intellectuals" and readers of the Daily Mail.

Day Eight

There is no Day Eight. The world will by now have been destroyed by a nuclear holocaust, which unleashes huge monsters from the ocean deep who bring a final end to civilisation as we knew it in the pre-Corbyn era.

"So you think I've gone a bit too far?"

TORIES AND LABOUR – THE DIFFERENCE

TORIES	LABOUR
Lose election to smarmy PR man (Blair)	Lose election to smarmy PR man (Cameron)
Appoint geek as leader (Hague)	Appoint geek as leader (Miliband)
Lose another election	Lose another election
Appoint troublesome backbencher as leader (IDS)	Appoint troublesome backbencher as leader (Corbyn)
Lose yet another election	Er...

Sun Exclusive
FIRST PICTURE OF JEREMY CORBYN'S SHADOW CABINET

Not enough men in it for my liking

Is This the End for Expert Analysis?

by Our Expert Analyst
Anna Lyst

IN the light of our failure to predict the result of the general election, the renaissance of left-wing politics under Jeremy Corbyn, and the crash of the unstoppable Chinese global juggernaut, expert analysts like me are beginning to wonder whether we are completely finished.

But, then again, why would you trust my opinion? After all, I was the one who wrote the piece "Another Coalition, Clegg Prepares for Power" in April, "Why Labour Will Shift to the Right" in May, and "The Yuan's the One: China Goes For Gold" last week.

So, perhaps we're not finished. Maybe we can rise Phoenix-like from the Ashes – which, incidentally, I predicted Australia would win 5-0.

Who knows? – certainly not me. It's idle to speculate, but it's a living. Honestly, I do try. (*You're fired, Ed*).

What?! I had no idea that was coming.

CORBYN SECURITY THREAT

Oh no, Cameron's secure for years!

GNOMEMART SPECIAL OFFER

THE Long To Rain Over Us

COMMEMORATIVE UMBRELLA

To mark the historic moment when Her Majesty Queen Elizabeth became the longest-reigning monarch in history, Gnomemart is proud to offer a lasting symbol of this unique record-breaking achievement.

Handmade by Taiwanese craftsmen, the 'Long To Rain Over Us' Commemorative Umbrella will continue to provide protection from the elements for as long as Her Majesty has served her people. Says TV weatherman Michael Fish, "You won't need this umbrella because it is never going to rain again – but as a mark of our affection for our longest-serving monarch, the 'Long To Rain Over Us'* brolly will remain an admired treasure in your hallway for generations to come."

PRICE: *Just £632.16*

Send money now to: Unit 94, The Pippa Middleton Trading Estate, Slough

*Rain not included